PHOTOGRAPHIC MANUAL OF WOODY LANDSCAPE PLANTS

Form and Function in the Landscape

MICHAEL A. DIRR

Director, University of
Georgia Botanical Gardens
Athens, Georgia

Sixth Printing, February, 1985

ISBN 0-87563-153-3

Published by
STIPES PUBLISHING COMPANY
10 - 12 Chester Street
Champaign, Illinois 61820

This book is dedicated to
My Parents
who taught me to observe, appreciate
and record the subtleties of the
plant world.

PREFACE

This book attempts to fill a gap in the area of ornamental horticulture and landscape architecture which for too long has been evident. The need for a reference text which encompasses photographs of plant habit and ornamental characteristics has been frequently brought to my attention. The first book, *Manual of Woody Landscape Plants*, Revised 1977, Stipes Publishing Co., has received wide acceptance as a plant materials text. One comment that kept surfacing was related to the absence of any photographs accompanying the text. This book is contructed along the lines of the first but includes only brief, terse descriptions of the various plants. The major thrust is geared towards black-and-white photographs. These photographs were selected to accurately represent form (growth habit) and other ornamental characteristics (flower, fruit, bark, unusual foliage). All photographs were taken by the author.

My hope is that this book will effectively complement the *Manual of Woody Landscape Plants* and allow students, nurserymen, homeowners and interested plantsmen the means by which they are better able to learn, appreciate and use landscape plants.

My sincere thanks to Leslie Spraker May for all her help, assistance and patience. This book might never have happened without her efforts.

The author would appreciate comments from interested readers concerning how the book might be improved in subsequent editions.

INTRODUCTION TO THE USE OF THE MANUAL

The plants are discussed and displayed in an alphabetical sequence by scientific name, much as in the format of the *Manual of Woody Landscape Plants*. If only the common name is known, the index will allow the reader to successfully locate the plant in question. The scientific names follow *Hortus III* in most instances, while common names were based on *Standardized Plant Names* and common sense.

The description accompanying each species usually contains a brief outline of the growth habit (form), foliage, bark, flower, fruit, culture, landscape use, size and hardiness (according to the Arnold Arboretum Hardiness Map, see page vi). Ornamental features are usually listed only if they are relatively prominent. For example, if fall color is not showy it is seldom discussed.

Each photograph is keyed numerically to the text for ready reference. Photographs attempt to depict typical growth habits and other features. Obviously, variation does occur and there is no practical way to compensate for all the variances that will be found in growth habit or other features. The principal idea is to introduce the reader to the typical growth habit of a particular plant and the more prominent ornamental characteristics. This should afford the reader an idea of how a particular plant may fit into a landscape situation. Verbal descriptions seldom do justice to the various plant characteristics. A photograph or, more ideally, face-to-plant confrontation are the ideal ways to effectively learn and assimilate information about a particular plant.

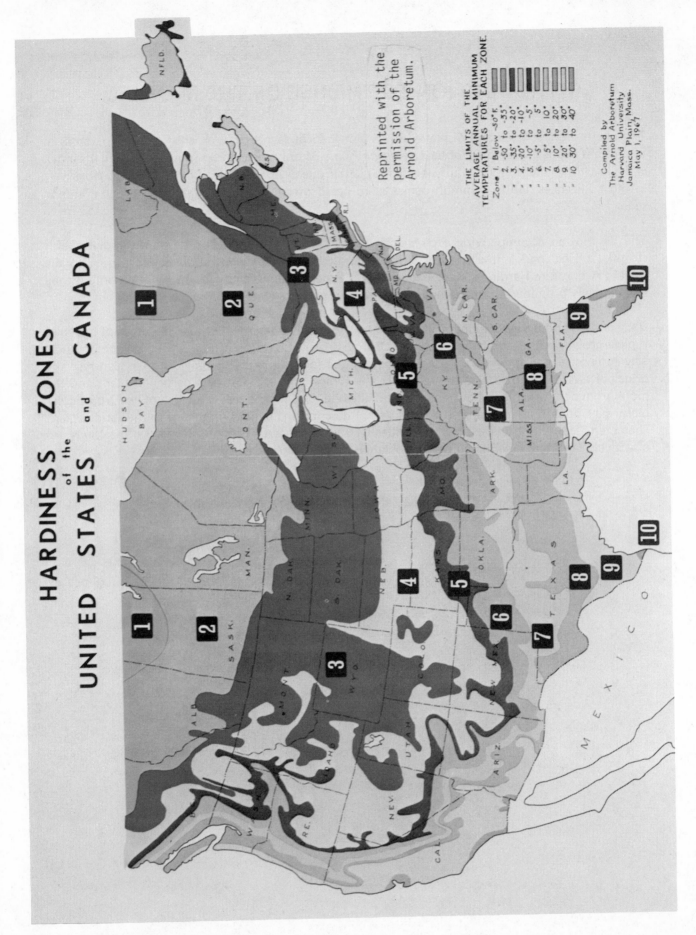

HARDINESS ZONES of the UNITED STATES and CANADA

Reprinted with the permission of the Arnold Arboretum.

THE LIMITS OF THE AVERAGE ANNUAL MINIMUM TEMPERATURES FOR EACH ZONE

Zone 1. Below -50°F.
2. -50° to -35°
3. -35° to -20°
4. -20° to -10°
5. -10° to -5°
6. -5° to 5°
7. 5° to 10°
8. 10° to 20°
9. 20° to 30°
10. 30° to 40°

Compiled by
The Arnold Arboretum
Harvard University
Jamaica Plain, Mass.
May 1, 1967

vi

Abelia x *grandiflora* — Glossy Abelia

1

2

Spreading, dense, rounded, multistemmed shrub with slightly drooping branches (1); often killed back in severe winters; dark, glossy green, summer foliage (2), bronze-purplish in fall; white-blushed pink flowers from July until frost; excellent for massing, hedging and grouping; 3 to 6' by 3 to 6'; Zone 5.

Abeliophyllum distichum — Korean Abelialeaf or White Forsythia

3

4

Multistemmed small shrub of rounded outline, developing arching branches (3); dark green summer foliage; white or faintly pink flowers on leafless stems in early April (4), fragrant; very lovely in early spring; nice plant for the shrub border; 3 to 5' by 3 to 4'; Zone 4.

Abies cilicica — Cilician Fir

5

Distinctly spire-like tree, almost obelisk-like with the angles rounded off (5); dark green needles with two bluish white bands beneath; prefers moist humid atmosphere; beautiful evergreen, especially in groupings; not for the small property; has withstood −25° F with no visible injury; 30 to 50' by 10 to 15'; Zone 5.

Abies concolor — Concolor or White Fir

6

Distinctly conical or spire-like in outline (6); like all firs presenting a rather stiff appearance to the landscape; needles vary from grayish green to bluish; the best fir for the midwest; performs better under hot dry conditions than other firs; 30 to 50' by 15 to 30'; 100' or greater in native haunts; Zone 4.

Abies procera —Noble Fir

7

Symmetrically pyramidal or narrowly conical in youth (7); mature trees develop a long, clear, columnar trunk with an essentially dome-like crown; dark bluish green needles, lower surface with two prominent, whitish bands; difficult to effectively use in small landscapes; acceptable for parks, golf courses and large areas; very handsome if properly grown; 50 to 75' by 20 to 30'; Zone 5.

Abies veitchii — Veitch Fir

8

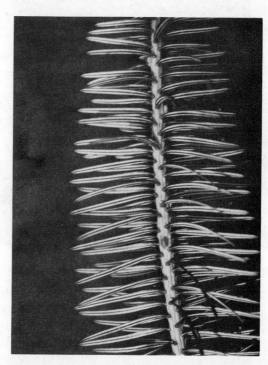

9

Broadly pyramidal evergreen tree, perhaps not as spire-like as the previous species (8); needles lustrous dark green above, with two chalky white bands beneath (9); handsome fir when young, loses some of its appeal with age; 50 to 75' by 25 to 35'; Zone 3.

Acanthopanax sieboldianus — Fiveleaf Aralia

10

11

Erect shrub with arching stems which eventually flop over to form a rounded outline (10); prominently suckering and spreading; bright green, pest-resistant foliage (11); adaptable to adverse conditions; makes a good barrier, hedge or screen for low maintenance areas; 8 to 10' by 8 to 10'; Zone 4.

Acer buergeranum — Trident Maple

12

13

Distinctly oval-rounded small tree of medium texture (12); glossy, dark green, summer foliage, changing to yellow, orange, red in fall; bark assumes a distinct orangish brown cast and develops a scaly character with maturity (13); good pest resistance; a fine small landscape or street tree ideally suited to lower midwest and east; 20 to 30' (40') by 15 to 25'; Zone 6, perhaps lower 5.

Acer campestre — Hedge Maple

14

15

16

Rounded in youth and old age (14, 15); often branched to the ground and must be limbed-up; dark green summer foliage, holding late in fall; very tolerant of dry and high-pH soils; withstands severe pruning; makes a good street or lawn specimen; 'Compactum' is a broad mounded form growing 3 to 4′ high (16); 25 to 35′ by 25 to 35′; can grow to 75′; Zone 4.

Acer cissifolium — Ivy-leaved Maple

A very beautiful and picturesquely branched tree developing a mushroom-like outline (17); the branches are low-slung and almost parallel with the ground (18); trifoliate leaves are medium (dark) green, change to yellow and red in fall; bark is soft gray and of smooth consistency; lovely, small, specimen tree, cannot recommend it highly enough; 20 to 30' with a slightly greater spread; Zone 5 (4).

Acer ginnala — Amur Maple

23

Large shrub or small tree of rounded outline (19); can be successfully tailored to specific landscape requirements by pruning; glossy dark green foliage, changing to yellow and red in fall; yellowish white fragrant flowers in late April or early May; red fruits on some plants; very adaptable maple (20); use as a small specimen or for hedging, screening, grouping (21); bark often a smooth gray on older branches; 'Durand Dwarf' (22) is a small, broad-rounded, shrubby form growing 4 to 6' by 8 to 10'; variety *semenovii* (23) is a compact bushy form, its leaves with deeper sinuses than the species and its overall texture more refined; species 15 to 18' with a similar spread; Zone 2.

Acer griseum — Paperbark Maple

26

One of the lovliest of all trees (24); oval to rounded outline; new foliage purplish, changing to dark green and finally russet-red in fall; bark is a beautiful cinnamon or red-brown and exfoliates in papery sheets (25); exfoliating characteristic starts on two to three-year-old branches (26); adaptable but difficult to propagate; exquisite tree, offering the landscape great seasonal beauty; small specimen tree which should be afforded a prominent place in the landscape; 20 to 30' with spread one-half of, or equal to, height; Zone 5 (4).

Acer japonicum — Fullmoon Maple

27

28

Closely allied to *A. palmatum*; shrubby bushy maple (27) with interesting foliage (28) and vivid yellow, orange-red fall coloration; requires considerable cultural attention; best used in shrub border; 20 to 30' high, but usually smaller, with equal spread; Zone 5.

Acer negundo — Box-Elder

29

30

Variable in outline; upright-oval to rounded, usually disheveled and straggly in appearance (29); considered an "alley cat" species; medium green foliage; grows anywhere; widely planted in plains and western mountain states because of adaptability to dry, high-pH soils; worthless in midwest and east as there are too many superior trees; 'Variegatum' (30) possesses white-margined foliage and is actually quite handsome, fruits are also variegated; 30 to 50' (70') with spread equal to, or greater than, height; Zone 2.

Acer nigrum — Black Maple

31

32

33

Similar to *A. saccharum* in most aspects; upright-oval to rounded in outline (31); dark green foliage, changing to golden yellow in fall; leaves often clasped (31) compared to flat-planed leaves of Sugar Maple; yellowish green flowers are borne in pendent clusters (32); 60 to 75' high; Zone 3.

Acer nikoense (now *A. maximowiczianum*) — Nikko Maple

34

35

Lovely, slow-growing, vase-shaped, round-headed, small tree (34); unusual trifoliate leaves (35) emerge bronze, change to medium green and finally glorious and spectacular yellow, brilliant red and purple in fall; bark is a smooth gray-brown; worthwhile tree for small landscapes; 20 to 30' by 20 to 30'; Zone 5.

Acer palmatum — Japanese Maple

36

37

38

39

40

41

One of the lovliest small maples; tends towards a rounded to broad-rounded character (36); often the branches assume a layered effect similar to *Cornus florida* (Flowering Dogwood); summer foliage (37) may be green, red, purple or variegated and is of unique shape; fall colors range from yellow to red; bark is essentially smooth, gray, showing slight vertical fissures (38, 39); not the easiest plant to grow; requires acid, moist, well-drained soils and protection from drying winds; variety *dissectum* (40) possesses finely cut foliage (41) and is usually mounded in outline, 8 to 10'; species may grow 15 to 25' (35') with a spread equal to, or greater than, height; Zones 5 to 6, depending on cultivar.

Acer platanoides — Norway Maple

42

43

44

45

46

47

Rounded, symmetrical in outline (42); dark green foliage changing to yellow-green or yellow in fall; showy yellow flowers (43) in April before the leaves; gray-black bark is distinctly ridged and furrowed (44); well-adapted culturally but does suffer from *Verticillium* wilt (45); widely used for shade, streets and parks; numerous cultivars including 'Erectum' (46), a distinctly upright-columnar form, and 'Globosum', which develops a dense lollipop-shaped outline (47); 40 to 50' with spread two-thirds of, or equal to, height; Zone 3.

Acer pseudoplatanus — Planetree Maple

48

49

Limitedly represented in the United States; develops upright spreading branches resulting in an oval to rounded outline (48); dark green summer foliage; bark often exfoliates in small scales exposing orangish brown inner bark (49); yellowish green flowers in May; very adaptable, quite tolerant of saline conditions; too many superior maples for this ever to become popular, might be used where salinity creates a cultural problem; 40 to 60' with spread two-thirds of, or equal to, height. Zone 5 (4).

Acer rubrum — Red Maple

50

51

52

54

53

In youth often pyramidal or elliptical, developing ascending branches which result in an irregular, ovoid or rounded crown (50); emerging leaves are reddish-tinged, changing to medium green and yellow to red in fall; bark is often smooth soft gray on young trees, scaly or slightly ridged and furrowed on old trees; flowers vary from yellow to red in late March or early April; male (51) and female (52) flowers often appearing in separate clusters; reddish fruits (53) in late April or May; relatively tolerant species but will not withstand high-pH soils; used extensively for modern-day landscaping of streets, parks, residences; may prove to be the next over-planted tree; 'Armstrong' (54) is a columnar form which can be effectively used in narrow planting areas; 40 to 60' with spread less than, or equal to, height; Zone 3.

Acer saccharinum — Silver Maple

55

56

57

Perhaps the worst of the maples; upright with bold spreading branches forming an oval to rounded crown (55); pendulous branchlets turn up at the ends; medium green summer foliage; gray-brown smooth bark on young trees; greenish yellow to red flowers in March (56); extremely fast-growing tree, weak wooded (57), lacks quality ornamental attributes; adaptable to wet and dry conditions; abhors high-pH situations; not recommended for modern landscapes—too big, clumsy and oafy; 50 to 70′ with spread about two-thirds the height and larger; Zone 3.

Acer saccharum — Sugar Maple

58

59

60

61

62

64

63

Perhaps the most spectacular of all maples; upright-oval to rounded in outline (58, 59) with boldly ascending branches (60); medium to dark green leaves turn excellent yellow to burnt orange and red in fall; handsome grayish brown bark (61); greenish yellow flowers (62) in April; excellent lawn or street tree, outstanding for fall color; 'Globosum' (63) is a round-headed form while 'Temple's Upright' ('Monumentale') (64) makes a handsome columnar specimen; 60 to 75' with a spread two-thirds of, or equal to, the height; Zone 3.

Acer sieboldianum — Siebold Maple

A rare but exquisite tree (65), the rich green foliage appearing as of borne in billowy clouds; somewhat rounded in outline; 20 to 25'; Zone 5.

Acer tataricum — Tatarian Maple

Closely allied to *A. ginnala*; rounded in outline (66); either low-branched or multistemmed; very clean tree; fruits (67) often develop excellent red or rose-red color in August; 20 to 30' with a comparable spread; Zone 4.

Acer tegmentosum — Manchu-striped Maple

One of the snake-barked maples; handsome small tree of obovate outline (68); bark is greenish, broken by vertical whitish fissures (69); very striking; 15 to 25'; Zone 4.

Acer truncatum — Purpleblow Maple

Small round-headed tree of neat outline with a regular branching pattern (70); young foliage is reddish purple, eventually dark glossy green and finally yellow-orange-red in fall; would make a lovely, small, specimen tree; 20 to 30' with a spread slightly less than, or equal to, height; Zone 5.

Actinidia arguta — Bower Actinidia

Vigorous, high climbing, twining vine which requires support (71); dark glossy green foliage (72); very rampant growing; performs well under less than ideal conditions; possibility for fast, but not obnoxious, cover; 30' plus; Zone 4.

Aesculus x *carnea* — Red Horsechestnut

74

75

A hybrid of *A. hippocastanum* x *A. pavia*; broad-spreading (73); dark glossy green foliage; fleshy pink to deep red flowers (74) in May; bark on old trunks (75) exfoliating; more resistant to scorch than *A. hippocastanum*; 30 to 40'; Zone 3.

Aesculus glabra — Ohio Buckeye

77

76

78

79

Rounded in youth (76) and at maturity (77); dark green foliage, developing yellow to brilliant orange-red to reddish brown color in fall; yellowish green flowers in May (78); fruits (79) are spiny dehiscent capsules; requires moist deep soils; scorch (leaves brown around the margins) is common in dry weather; one of the first trees to leaf out in spring and drop in fall; handsome in a native situation; 30 to 40' (50') with a similar spread; Zone 3.

Aesculus hippocastanum — Common Horsechestnut

81

82

83

84

85

Pyramidal-oval (80) to rounded (81) in outline; highly variable in growth habit; dark green foliage (82) holding late, although often covered with mildew and blotch; bark often becomes scaly, platy and the entire trunk develops a slight spiral; lovely, large, upright panicles of white flowers (84) in May; not a good tree for small residences but fine for parks and other large areas; 'Baumanni' (85) has double white flowers which last longer than those of the species and produce no fruits; 50 to 75' by 40 to 70'; Zone 3.

Aesculus octandra — Yellow Buckeye

86

87

Distinctly upright-oval in outline, almost rectangular with the corners rounded off (86); foliage and flowers somewhat similar to Ohio Buckeye; the gray bark (87) develops large flakes and makes for an interesting mosaic; perhaps the lovliest of the large *Aesculus*, certainly worth considering for parks, campuses and golf courses; 50 to 75' with a spread of two-thirds the height; Zone 3.

Aesculus parviflora — Bottlebrush Buckeye

88

89

Under-rated shrubby buckeye; tends to sucker and form colonies (88); dark green summer foliage, yellow in fall; feathery white flowers (89) in July; adaptable and extremely shade-tolerant; fine plant for under trees or anyplace shade presents a cultural problem; free of the problems which afflict *A. glabra* and *A. hippocastanum*; 8 to 12' by 8 to 15' and greater; Zone 4.

Aesculus pavia — Red Buckeye

90

91

92

A small, clump-forming, round-topped shrub or small tree (90); handsome, reddish-tinged, new foliage (91) changing to lustrous dark green; bright red flowers (92) in May; worthwhile addition to the garden; cheerfully accompanies *A. parviflora* in any landscape; 10 to 20' (30'), spreading that much or more; Zone 4.

Ailanthus altissima — Tree of Heaven

94

93

A large, coarse, spreading, open tree of gaunt outline (93, 94); can be shrubby under certain conditions; dark green foliage; yellow-green flowers in June with the male especially vile smelling; will grow and proliferate about anywhere; should only be used where nothing else will grow; coarse and unappealing — a weed; 40 to 60' with an extremely variable spread; Zone 4.

Akebia quinata — Fiveleaf Akebia

95

96

97

Unusual vine, seldom seen in American gardens (95); requires support; handsome bluish green foliage (96); female flowers are chocolate-purple (97), staminate rose-purple; a vigorous vine, will cover large areas; semi-evergreen if properly sited; 20 to 40'; Zone 4.

Albizia julibrissin — Albizia, Silk-tree or Mimosa

98

99

100

Somewhat vase-shaped, broad-spreading, often with several trunks, forming a flat-topped crown (98); dark green foliage (99); powder-puff pinkish flowers (100) from June through frost; lack of hardiness limits use in north — widely planted in southwest, however; suffers from vascular wilt disease; withstands alkalinity, dry conditions; 25 to 35' by 25 to 35'; Zone 6.

Alnus cordata — Italian Alder

102

101

Distinctly pyramidal tree in youth and maturity (101); lustrous dark green foliage; large fruit structures (1″ long) which persist through winter (102); widely adaptable to differing soil conditions — wet, dry, fertile, infertile; perhaps preferable to *Alnus glutinosa* but seldom seen in modern landscapes; 30 to 50' by 20 to 30'; Zone 5.

Alnus glutinosa — Common, Black or European Alder

104

103

105

Tree of weak pyramidal outline, at times developing an ovoid or oblong head of irregular proportions (103); dark green foliage holding late into fall; male flowers in pendulous cylindrical catkins while females are borne in ovoid cone-like structures (104); very tolerant of wet and dry conditions; can become weedy, as it seeds freely at a young age; good plant for intertile soils; 'Fastigiata' (105) is an excellent upright cultivar; 40 to 60' by 20 to 40'; Zone 3.

Amelanchier arborea — Downy Serviceberry, also called Juneberry, Shadbush, Service-tree or Sarvis-tree

106

108

107

109

Multistemmed shrub (106) or low-branched small tree (107) with a rounded crown; foliage (108) is grayish when emerging, changes to medium green in summer, yellow apricot orange, and dull, deep, dusty red in fall; grayish bark streaked with slight longitudinal fissures, very handsome (109); exquisite, soft-textured, white flowers in April; bloomy, red to purplish black, sweetish fruits in June; adaptable to varied soils and climates; nice specimen, patio plant, good for groupings or naturalizing; 15 to 25' (40'), spread is quite variable but often equal to height; Zone 4.

Amelanchier canadensis — Shadblow Serviceberry

110

111

Often confused with *A. arborea* but much more upright and spreads by means of suckers from the base (110, 111); apparently more tolerant of wet soil than *A. arborea*; 10 to 20' (25') high; Zone 4.

Amelanchier x *grandiflora* — Apple Serviceberry

A naturally occuring hybrid between *A. arborea* and *A. laevis*; young leaves purplish and pubescent; flowers often larger or longer, with more slender racemes than parents and tinged pink in bud; 15 to 25' high; Zone 4.

Amelanchier laevis — Allegheny Serviceberry

113

112

Closely allied to *A. arborea* but differing by virtue of the bronze purple color of the unfolding leaves and their lack of pubescence (hairs) (112, 113); 15 to 25' by 15 to 25'; Zone 4.

Amelanchier stolonifera — Running Serviceberry

114

A small stoloniferous shrub (114) forming thickets of stiff erect stems; fruit is sweet, juicy and of good flavor; the fruits of serviceberries are better than blueberries; 4 to 6'; Zone 4.

Amorpha fruticosa — Indigobush Amorpha

115

Definitely not the best shrub ever invented; ungainly, developing a leggy character, with the bulk of the bright green foliage on the upper one-third of the plant (115); main asset is the tolerance to poor, dry, sandy soils; almost weed-like if used in good soils; 6 to 20' by 5 to 15', depending on soil conditions; Zone 4.

Ampelopsis brevipedunculata — Porcelain Ampelopsis

116   117

Vine (116), climbing by tendrils, not as dense or vigorous as *Actinidia*; rich green foliage; fruit changes from pale lilac and yellow to a robin's-egg-blue; very adaptable but best in full sun; interesting plant for fruit effect, could be used on a trellis or fence with success; 'Elegans' (117) shows white and pink leaf-mottling; 10 to 15' (25'); Zone 4.

Aralia spinosa — Devil's-walkingstick, Hercules-Club

118

120

119

A rather interesting native species developing as a few-stemmed large shrub or small tree; usually forming thickets because of the ability to freely sucker from roots (118); medium to dark green foliage changing to yellow in fall; white flowers in July-August (119); blackish fruits, the stalks of which turn pinkish red and are effective into September; thrives with neglect, prefers moist well-drained soils; stems are quite spiny (120); good plant for difficult sites — highway right-of-ways, poor soil areas; 10 to 20' (30'), spreading indefinitely if not controlled; Zone 4.

Arctostaphylos uva-ursi — Bearberry, Kinnikinick

121

122

Low-growing, glossy-leaved, evergreen, ground cover, forming broad thick mats (121); bronze to reddish in fall; white-tinged pink flowers in April-May followed by persistent red fruit in August (122); thrives in poor, sandy, infertile soils; has been called "the prettiest, sturdiest and most reliable ground cover"; 6 to 12" by 2 to 4'; Zone 2.

Aronia arbutifolia — Red Chokeberry

123

124

Distinctly upright, weakly spreading, multistemmed shrub, somewhat open, leggy and round-topped (123); lustrous deep green foliage, rich crimson or purplish red in fall; white flowers in May followed by bright red, showy, persistent fruits (124); adaptable to wet and dry soils; excellent for fruit effect, however, plant is somewhat leggy; use in groups and masses; 6 to 10' by 3 to 5'; Zone 5 (4).

Aronia melanocarpa — Black Chokeberry

125

Similar to *A. arbutifolia*, however, tends to sucker profusely and forms large colonies (125); fruit is black; well-adapted to wet and dry soils; 3 to 5′ (8′) and spreading indefinitely; Zone 4.

Asimina triloba — Pawpaw

126

127

128

Multistemmed shrub or small tree (126) with short trunk and spreading branches forming a dense pyramidal or round-topped head; dark green foliage changes to yellow in fall (127); lurid purple flowers (128) in May on leafless branches; banana-cantaloupe-tasting, yellow-green to blackish fruits; prefers deep moist soils and partial shade; interesting, best used in naturalizing; 15 to 20' (35') with spread equal to height; Zone 5.

Berberis candidula — Paleleaf Barberry

129

130

Low-growing, very dense, evergreen shrub of hemispherical to rounded outline with the outer branches rigidly arching (129); excellent in masses, as a grouping or facer plant; handsome lustrous foliage; yellow flowers (130) and purplish berries; 2 to 4' high, spreading to 5'; Zone 5.

Berberis chenaultii — Chenault Barberry

131

One of the best evergreen barberries (131) for northern areas because of vigorous growth and good condition of the foliage through winter; 3 to 4'; Zone 5.

Berberis julianae — Wintergreen Barberry

132

133

134

135

An upright, eventually rounded, semi-evergreen shrub (132) of spiny consistency; lustrous dark green foliage (133) changing to wine-red in fall; handsome yellow flowers in May; good barrier, mass, screen — difficult to penetrate (134); 'Nana' (135) grows one-half the size of the species; 6 to 10' by 6 to 10'; Zone 5, actually better in 6.

Berberis koreana — Korean Barberry

136

137

138

Multistemmed oval to "haystack"-shaped plant (136) of rather dense constitution; often suckers and may become unruly in habit; foliage medium green, developing rich reddish purple color in fall and staying effective into November; yellow, 3 to 4" long, racemose flowers (137) in May followed by red fruits (138) which persist late into fall and winter; adaptable; excellent plant for shrub border, masses, low screens; 4 to 6', slightly less in spread; Zone 4.

Berberis x mentorensis — Mentor Barberry

139

140

Hybrid between *B. julianae* x *B. thunbergii*; upright, stiff, with many slender stems, becoming bushy with age, very regular in outline (139); leathery, dark green, semi-evergreen foliage; extremely adaptable; excellent for hedges, masses, barriers (140); 5 to 7' by 5 to 7'; Zone 5.

Berberis thunbergii — Japanese Barberry

141

142

143

144

145

146

The most popular barberry; many-branched, very dense, rounded shrub, usually broader than tall (141); medium green summer foliage, changing to reddish purple in fall—often quite variable; small yellow flowers in April, followed by bright red, egg-shaped fruits which persist through winter (142); very adaptable, withstands dry conditions; used in groupings, massing and as hedges and barriers (143); 'Crimson Pygmy' (144) is a drawf compact form with reddish purple foliage, 8-year old plants being only 2' by 3'; 'Erecta' (145) is an upright compact form which makes a good hedge; 'Kobold' (146) is a dwarf (1-1/2 by 2 to 3') form with rich green foliage; species 3 to 6' by 4 to 7'; Zone 4.

Berberis verruculosa — Warty Barberry

147

Similar to *B. candidula* but not as hardy (0 to −5°F); makes a dense, mounded, evergreen shrub (147); excellent, lustrous, dark green foliage; 3 to 6' high; Zone 6.

Betula alleghaniensis — Yellow Birch

148

149

Pyramidal in youth, rounded with time (148); dull, dark green foliage, changing to yellow in fall; bark (149) is yellowish bronze and sheds in papery strips; prefers moist cool soils and cool summer temperatures; good choice for northern areas; 60 to 75' in height with a similar spread; Zone 3.

Betula lenta — Sweet, Black or Cherry Birch

150

151

Pyramidal and dense in youth, forming an irregular, rounded, sometimes wide-spreading crown at maturity (150); deep, dark green foliage changing to fantastic golden yellow in fall; bark grayish to brownish black (151) and breaking into large, thin, irregular, scaly plates; requires deep, moist, slightly acid, well-drained soils for best growth; exquisite tree for parks, campuses, golf courses; the best birch for fall color; 40 to 50' by 35 to 45' (55'); Zone 3.

Betula maximowicziana — Monarch Birch

152

153

154

A birch of the future but somewhat horticulturally confused; habit is rounded and mop-like in out-line (152); lustrous, dark green foliage (153), changing to clear butter-yellow in fall; bark may be gray, whitish or orangish brown and cling to the tree in shaggy masses (154); would make a hand-some specimen tree for large areas; 40 to 50' high; Zone 4.

Betula nigra — River Birch

156

155

157

158

Pyramidal to oval-headed in youth (155), often rounded at maturity (156); lustrous, medium green foliage; at best, poor yellow in fall; exfoliating bark (157) which ranges from gray-brown to cinnamon or reddish brown in color; spectacular for winter effect (158); very tolerant of wet soils and inhabits water courses over its native range; will not withstand high-pH situations; beautiful tree for groupings, parks, golf courses, campuses; disappointing for fall color; 40 to 70' by 40 to 60'; Zone 4.

Betula papyrifera — Paper, Canoe Birch

159

160

161

162

Loosely pyramidal in youth (159), developing an irregular, oval to rounded crown at maturity (160); dark green foliage, changing to a good yellow in fall; bark is a beautiful white, peeling (161) with age and finally developing blackened areas (162); best adapted to colder climates; prefers moist, acid, well-drained soils; excellent specimen tree; beautiful in a native situation; not as susceptible to borer as *B. pendula*; 50 to 70' with a spread equal to one-half or two-thirds the height; Zone 2.

Betula pendula — European White Birch

163

164

165

166

Often sold as "White Birch"; gracefully pyramidal in youth (163), developing an oval-pyramidal to oval-rounded outline; glossy, dark green foliage, changing to yellow in fall; not a good fall-coloring tree in the midwest; bark is a good white in youth (164), developing black fissured areas in old age (165); tremendously susceptible to bronze birch borer; 'Dalecarlica' (166) is a graceful, cut-leaf form, having more pendulous branches than the species and developing a rounded outline; 40 to 50' by 20 to 30'; Zone 2.

Betula platyphylla — Asian White Birch

167

168

Interesting tree because of resistance to bronze birch borer; pyramidal in youth (167), perhaps becoming more open with age; lustrous, dark green foliage, yellow in fall; bark is a good white and maintains that color in old age (168); might prove a valuable tree in the future because of resistance to bronze birch borer; presently not well known, but some nurserymen are starting to grow the species; good specimen; 40 to 50′ high with variable spread; Zone 4.

Betula populifolia — Gray Birch

169

170

Narrow, irregularly open, conical crown with slender branches which are often pendulous (169); dark, glossy green leaves, changing to yellow in fall; bark is a dusty white (170); adaptable to dry, sandy, rocky, infertile soils; best for naturalizing or rough area use; 20 to 30′ (40′) high, spread 10 to 20′; Zone 3.

Buddleia alternifolia — Fountain Butterfly-bush

Wide-spreading shrub with fountain-like outline; dull, gray-green summer foliage; handsome, lilac-purple flowers are borne in long spikes in mid-May; thrives in infertile but well-drained, gravelly or sandy soils; the branches are not killed to the ground in cold weather as is the case with *B. davidii* cultivars; makes a nice addition to the shrub border; must have ample room to spread; 8 to 12′ by 15′; Zone 5.

Buddleia davidii — Orange-eye Butterfly-bush

171

172

In the northern states the plant reacts as an herbaceous perennial and dies to the ground; the habit is usually oval to rounded (171); summer foliage is dark green above with grayish pubescence beneath; flowers range from bluish purple with orange centers in the species, to white, pink, red, purple and blue in the cultivars, are fragrant and occur from July through frost, providing spectacular late season color; butterflies constantly hover about the blooms (172); the flowers are borne on new growth and pruning should be accomplished in early spring; prefers full sun and a well-drained soil that has been liberally supplemented with organic matter; best used in shrub border where color is often lacking in summer months; 6 to 8′ in northern climates, reaching 15 to 20′ in southern gardens; Zone 5.

Buxus microphylla var. *koreana* — Korean Littleleaf Box or Boxwood

173

174

175

Much-branched, compact, dense, rounded or broad-rounded evergreen shrub (173); medium green foliage, changing to a sickly yellow-green-brown in winter; used for foundation plantings, massing (174), edging situations and, most appropriately, for hedges (175); var. *koreana* represents the hardy form and, along with the cultivars 'Tide Hill' and 'Wintergreen', should be used in northern areas; 3 to 4' by 3 to 4'; Zone 4.

Buxus sempervirens — Common Box or Boxwood

176

177

178

Dense, multibranched, evergreen shrub of rounded or broad-rounded outline, holding its foliage to the ground (176); dark green foliage throughout the year; extremely popular in east and south for hedges, foundations, topiary work; a comparison of the two boxwoods is offered in photograph 177; 'Vardar Valley' (178) is a flat-topped, dense, low-growing form with good, dark green foliage all winter and excellent hardiness; 15 to 20' high with an equal or greater spread; Zone 5 or 6, depending on cultivar.

Callicarpa japonica — Japanese Beautyberry

179

180

181

Bushy rounded shrub with arching branches (179); medium green summer foliage; small, pinkish white flowers in July (180); violet to metallic-purple fruits in fall (181); not particularly hardy and should be sited in a protected area; unusual because of fruit color; good for shrub border; 4 to 6' by 4 to 6'; Zone 5, probably best in 6.

Calluna vulgaris — Scotch Heather

182

183

One of the most beautiful ground covers; upright-branching, low-growing, evergreen ground cover with densely leafy, ascending branches forming thick mats (182); rich, medium green foliage, often bronzing in fall; dainty, rosy to purplish pink flowers in July through September; ideal for rock garden (183); requires acid, moist, well-drained soils, preferably of low fertility; 4 to 24''; Zone 4.

Calocedrus decurrens — California Incensecedar
(formerly *Libocedrus decurrens*)

184

185

Stiff, narrow-columnar, evergreen tree in youth; regular in outline and with a distinct formal character even in old age (184); foliage is a lustrous dark green; bark (185) is a cinnamon-red-brown;
handsome specimen for large areas, perhaps as a tall hedge; very formal, therefore difficult to use;
30 to 50' by 8 to 10', can grow 125 to 150' in the wild; Zone 5.

Calycanthus floridus — Common Sweetshrub, Carolina Allspice or Strawberry Shrub

186

187

188

189

Dense, bushy, rounded or broad-rounded shrub of regular outline (186, 187); dark green foliage,
often glossy, yellowish in fall but not effective; reddish brown, strawberry-banana-scented flowers
in May (188, 189); adaptable, does well in shade; nice plant for shrub border, perhaps useful for
massing, grouping; 6 to 9' by 6 to 12'; Zone 4.

Campsis radicans — Common Trumpetcreeper

190

191

A rampant-growing, clinging, twining vine; bright green, pest-resistant foliage; handsome, orange-red, trumpet-shaped flowers from July through September (190); winter habit is rather gaunt (191); will grow under almost any conditions; the hybrid 'Mme. Galen' has larger and brighter colored flowers than the species; 30 to 50', essentially limited only by the size of the structure upon which it is growing; Zone 4.

Caragana arborescens — Siberian Peashrub

192

193

194

195

196

Usually an erect-oval shrub, however, can develop a rounded outline (192); bright green foliage (193); yellow flowers in May (194), not particularly showy; very durable plant, extremely cold-hardy; tolerates wind and dry alkaline soil; used in plains states for hedges, screens, windbreaks; 'Lorbergii' (195) has finely cut leaves, resulting in a rather feathery overall appearance; 'Pendula' (196) is a delicate weeping form with more ornamental appeal than the species; 15 to 20' by 12 to 18'; Zone 2.

Carpinus betulus — European Hornbeam

197

198

199

200

201

202

203

Limitedly represented in this country; makes a massive oval to rounded, low-branched, muscle-barked tree of indescribable beauty (197, 198); foliage is dark green, inconsistently yellow in fall; tolerates a wide range of soil conditions—light to heavy, acid to alkaline; prefers well-drained situations; 'Columnaris' (199) is a densely branched and foliaged, spire-like, slow-growing tree, usually maintaining a central leader; 'Fastigiata' (200, 201) is somewhat of a misnomer, for the cultivar develops an oval shape and reaches 30 to 40' in height, makes an excellent unpruned screen (202); 'Globosa' (203) is rounded in outline without a central leader; the species will grow 40 to 60' high and as wide; Zone 4.

Carpinus caroliniana — American Hornbeam, also called Blue Beech, Ironwood, Musclewood

204

205

206

207

Small, multistemmed, bushy shrub or single-stemmed tree (204) with a wide-spreading, flat or round-topped crown; exquisitely handsome when properly grown (205); dark green foliage, changing to yellow, orange and red in fall; bark is slate-gray, relatively smooth, irregularly fluted (206, 207); requires cool, moist, well-drained soils for best growth; interesting tree for naturalized-type landscapes, perhaps small residential properties; 20 to 30' high and as wide; Zone 2.

Carya illinoinensis — Pecan

208

Largest of the *Carya* group; usually tall and straight with a uniform, symmetrical, broadly oval crown (208); dark green summer foliage; nuts are valuable as food for man and animal; prefers deep, moist, well-drained soils; extremely difficult to transplant; of limited value for landscaping; 70 to 100' (and larger) by 40 to 70'; Zone 5.

Carya ovata — Shagbark Hickory

209

210

Usually a high-branching tree with a straight slender trunk and narrow oblong crown of spreading branches, the lower drooping, the upper ascending (209); deep green foliage, rich yellow to golden brown fall color; bark (210) is gray to brown and breaks into thin plates which are free at the end and attached in the middle; difficult to transplant; very beautiful in native setting; 60 to 80' by 40 to 60'; Zone 4.

Castanea dentata — American Chestnut

211

213

212

Once a dominant tree of the eastern American forests, chestnut blight has essentially eliminated it from the landscape; develops a deep, broad-rounded crown (211); the fruits are enclosed within a prickly involucre (212); bark is a handsome grayish black with flat gray ridges interspersed with darker furrowed areas (213); obviously not a tree for the modern garden but worth remembering; Zone 4.

Castanea mollissima — Chinese Chestnut

214

Tree of rounded outline, usually as broad as tall (214); limitedly grown for ornament; lustrous, dark green summer foliage; creamy white flowers in June; the sweet nuts are valuable; resistant to the dreaded chestnut blight (*Endothia parasitica*); might prove useful to the hobbyist-type gardener; 40 to 60' by 40 to 60'; Zone 4.

Catalpa bignonioides — Southern Catalpa

215

216

217

Broadly rounded in outline with an irregular crown (215) composed of short crooked branches; medium green summer foliage; best reserved for lower midwest and southern states; a very coarse tree, maximally attractive in flower (white-spotted purple in June); bark is often scaly (216), exfoliating in small plates; very adaptable; 'Nana' (217) is a bushy, 3 to 6' high, pom-pom type which rarely, if ever, flowers and is often grafted on the species; 30 to 40' tall and as wide; Zone 4.

Catalpa speciosa — Northern Catalpa, also called Western or Hardy Catalpa

218

219

220

Tree with a narrow, open, irregular, oval crown (218); out-of-place in the residential landscape; very coarse; medium to dark green summer foliage; flowers similar to those of *C. bignonioides* but two weeks earlier; long fruits (219) are interesting but messy, have resulted in another common name—"Cigar Tree"; the bark is a grayish brown on old trunks (220), usually exhibiting a ridged and furrowed characteristic; 40 to 60' high (sometimes 100') by 20 to 40'; Zone 4.

Cedrela sinensis — Chinese Cedrela or Toon

221

222

Single or multiple-stemmed tree or large shrub of oval to rounded proportions (221); I have seen four specimens around the country and every one looked different; resembles *Ailanthus* in leaf and coarseness; bark peels off in strips (222); interesting plant; 30 to 40'; Zone 5.

Cedrus atlantica — Atlas Cedar

223

224

225

A large, widely pyramidal evergreen tree with an upright leader and spreading horizontal branches (223); becoming more flat-topped in old age; needles range from light green to silvery blue in color; a handsome specimen tree of unrivaled distinction; 'Glauca' (224) has intense bluish white foliage and is preferable to the species, while 'Glauca Pendula' (225) is a weeping form of 'Glauca' with the branches cascading like water over rocks; 40 to 60' by 30 to 50'; Zone 6.

Cedrus deodara — Deodar Cedar

226

227

Broadly pyramidal when young with gracefully pendulous branchlets (226); perhaps the lovliest of the true cedars; bluish green foliage is attractive; makes a choice specimen plant (227); the cultivars 'Kashmir' and 'Kingsville' are supposedly hardy to −25°F, however, have not performed well in −10°F weather in Illinois; 40 to 70'; Zone 7.

Cedrus libani — Cedar-of-Lebanon

228

229

230

Pyramidal in youth; with age a stately tree (228), massive of trunk with wide-spreading branches, the lower ones sweeping the ground; lustrous, dark green needles; slender male cones are borne upright all over the branches (229), while the oval woody female cones are borne higher up in the tree (230); another choice specimen plant where it can be grown; all *Cedrus* require well-drained soils and freedom from sweeping drying winds; 40 to 60', however, can grow 75 to 120'; Zone 6.

Celastrus scandens — American Bittersweet

232

231

Vigorous twining vine (231), engulfing every structure in its path; glossy, dark green foliage; principal value is the crimson-yellow fruit (232) which is used in table decorations; need male and female plants for fruit set; tolerant of most soil conditions; needs room in the landscape; 30 to 40'; Zone 2.

Celtis laevigata — Sugar Hackberry or Sugar-berry

233

Rounded to broad-rounded tree with spreading, often pendulous branches (233); foliage is usually lustrous dark green; fruits are orange-red to blue-black and relished by birds; very adaptable, withstanding extremes of soil conditions; used extensively in the south on streets, in parks and other large areas; not as popular as *C. occidentalis* in northern states; 60 to 80' and as wide; Zone 5.

Celtis occidentalis — Common Hackberry

234

235

236

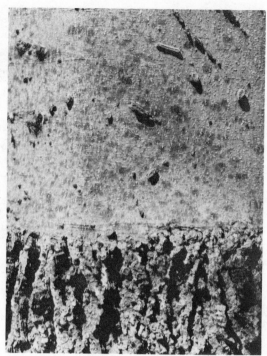

237

In youth weakly pyramidal (234); in old age the crown is oval to rounded with ascending arching branches (235), often with drooping branchlets; unfortunately, extremely variable in growth habit, and seedling-grown trees exhibit ridiculous variation; foliage is not as handsome as *C. laevigata*; fruit a fleshy, orange-red to dark purple drupe (236); bark develops corky warts or ridges compared to relatively smooth bark of *C. laevigata* (see 237, where Sugar is grafted on Common Hackberry); very durable tree and will withstand poor soils and winds; 40 to 60'; Zone 2.

Cercidiphyllum japonicum — Katsuratree

239

238

240

241

Either strongly pyramidal (238) or wide-spreading (239) in habit; new foliage a beautiful reddish purple, maturing to bluish green (240), turning yellow to red in fall; bark is brownish and slightly shaggy on old trunks (241); very pest-resistant tree; requires considerable moisture, especially during establishment; lovely specimen tree, ideal for residential properties, parks, golf courses, campuses, large areas; 40 to 60'; variable in spread; Zone 4.

Cercis canadensis — Eastern Redbud

242

244

243

246

245

247

Usually a small tree with the trunk divided close to the ground and forming a spreading, flat-topped to rounded crown (242); new growth reddish purple, gradually changing to a dark, often somewhat lustrous green, finally exhibiting yellow or yellow-green fall color; the lovely rose-pink (with purplish tinge) flowers are borne on leafless stems (243) and often are evident on large trunks (244); old trunks (245) provide aesthetic appeal; variety *alba* (246) is a white-flowering type and 'Plena' (247) is a double, rose-pink form; all serve as functional small specimens, in groupings and as shrub, border plants; 20 to 30' by 25 to 35'; Zone 4.

Cercis chinensis — Chinese Redbud

248

249

A multistemmed shrub of somewhat irregular proportions (248, 249); does not compare aesthetical-ly to our native species, however, the flowers (rosy purple) appear more vivid and are borne about a week later; best reserved for the southern and eastern areas; to 10'; Zone 6.

Chaenomeles japonica — Japanese Floweringquince

250

251

Low-growing, broad-spreading shrub (250); forming an interlacing network of thorny stems (251); flowers are orange-red; too many better shrubs; unequivocally a "garbage can" shrub; 3'; Zone 4.

Chaenomeles speciosa — Common Floweringquince

252

254

253

255

A shrub of rounded outline (252), broad-spreading with a tangled and dense twiggy mass of more or less spiny branches; some forms erect, others quite rambling; quite variable due to hybridization with *C. japonica*; foliage is bronzy red when emerging, becoming glossy dark green at maturity; double or single flowers (253, 254), good color range, including white, pink, orange and scarlet; fruits are yellow-green or blushed reddish (255); best used in shrub border; in wet weather often defoliated by a leaf disease; somewhat of a "garbage can" shrub but very popular because of flowers; 6 to 10' by 6 to 10'; Zone 4.

Chamaecyparis nootkatensis — Nootka Falsecypress

256

257

Develops a conical crown composed of numerous drooping branches (256) with long, pendulous, flattened sprays; evergreen needles are dark bluish green; not extensively seen in cultivation; requires cool, moist, humid atmosphere and root-run for best growth; 'Pendula' (257) is a handsome weeping form; 30 to 45' high (60 to 90' in the wild); Zone 4.

Chamaecyparis obtusa — Hinoki Falsecypress

259

258

260

A tall, slender, evergreen pyramid (258) with spreading branches and drooping, frond-like branch-lets; lustrous, dark green foliage; principally represented in cultivation by the numerous cultivars; 'Nana Gracilis' (259) has thick, dark green foliage and a globular outline; 'Pendula' (260) is a grace-fully weeping form with strongly pendulous branchlets; all prefer moist humid climate and moist, cool, well-drained soil; very lovely and valuable landscape plant; species will grow 50 to 75'; Zone 4.

Chamaecyparis pisifera 'Plumosa' — Plume Sawara or Japanese Falsecypress

261

262

Pyramidal tree with a loose open outline (unless pruned as in 261) and numerous sprays thickly covered with slender feathery branchlets; many other interesting cultivars within the species; 'Filifera' (262) has drooping stringy branches and forms a dense mound, usually no higher than 6 to 8'; species 50 to 70'; Zone 3.

Chionanthus retusus — Chinese Fringetree

263

264

265

Usually a multistemmed large shrub of rounded proportions (263); lustrous, leathery, dark green summer foliage; white fleecy flowers in May-June (264); blue-black fruits; interesting grayish brown bark which becomes more intriguing when adequately exposed (265); handsome specimen or shrub border plant; 15 to 25' and as wide; Zone 5, best in 6.

Chionanthus virginicus — White Fringetree

266

267

268

Difficult to imagine a more beautiful shrub in flower; spreading, rather open habit, often wider than high (266); beautiful, white, fragrant flowers borne in 6 to 8'' long, fleecy, soft-textured panicles (267) in May-June; dark blue fruit borne prolifically on female plants (268); prefers deep, moist, acid soil; very slow-growing in clay soils of midwest; good plant for shrub border; 12 to 20' and as wide; Zone 4.

Cladrastis lutea — American Yellowwood

269

271

270

272

Usually a low-branching tree with a broad-rounded crown (269, 270) of delicate branches; superb, bright green summer foliage; yellow fall color; handsome, fragrant, white flowers (extremely showy about one out of three years) (271); gray, beech-like bark (272); very adaptable, worthy specimen tree; 30 to 50′ by 40 to 55′; Zone 5.

Clematis species and hybrids

273

274

275

276

A handsome group of flowering vines, clinging by twining stems and petioles; excellent for covering fences (273), trellises (274), rock piles; the species types, such as *C. texensis* (275), differ significantly from the large-flowered hybrids (276); require considerable cultural care and a moist, cool, well-drained root zone; 5 to 6' (18') on the appropriate structure; Zone 4.

Clethra alnifolia — Summersweet Clethra

278

277

Erect-growing, dense, leafy shrub of oval to rounded outline (277) with a slight suckering tendency; handsome, deep green summer foliage, limitedly yellow in fall; white, deliciously fragrant, July-August flowers (278), nice for scenting the garden; withstands wet soils; 3 to 8' by 4 to 6'; Zone 3.

Clethra barbinervis — Cinnamon Clethra

279

Larger growing than *C. alnifolia* with similar foliage and flowers; bark is a polished cinnamon color and very ornamental; can be grown as multistemmed shrub (279) or small tree; to 18'; Zone 5.

Colutea arborescens — Common Bladder-senna

280

Rounded shrub of dense habit (280); rich green, pest-resistant foliage; flowers yellow with red markings, May through July; fruit is a bladder-like, 3'' long pod; very accommodating, performing well under most conditions; good filler in poor soil areas where more ornamental shrubs will not grow; 10 to 12'; Zone 5.

Comptonia peregrina — Sweetfern

281

Shrub with slender, often erect branches, developing a broad, flat-topped to rounded outline as it suckers and colonizes (281); lustrous, dark green foliage; prefers peaty, sandy, sterile, acid soils; has ability to fix nitrogen; good plant for stabilizing banks, cuts and fills along highways; 2 to 4' by 4 to 8'; Zone 2.

Cornus alba — Tatarian Dogwood, also called Red-stemmed Dogwood

282

283

284

Usually distinctly erect in youth, arching somewhat with age (282); medium to dark green foliage, changing to reddish purple in fall; white, limitedly ornamental flowers in May-June; whitish fruits (283); principal landscape asset is the red stem color which is brashly evident during the winter months; 'Argenteo-marginata' (284) offers a white-margined leaf; best used in groupings or masses; 8 to 10' by 5 to 10'; Zone 2.

Cornus alternifolia — Pagoda Dogwood

285

286

287

Spreading, horizontal, low-branched tree or shrub with an interesting stratified outline (285); dark green foliage, changing to reddish purple in fall; white flowers (286) in May-June; interesting red (changing to bluish black) fruits (287) highlight the plant in summer; excellent for the shrub border or where horizontal lines are needed in the landscape; 15 to 25', possibly one to one and one-half times that in spread; Zone 3.

Cornus amomum — Silky Dogwood

288

289

Rounded multistemmed shrub, usually twiggy and round-topped in youth (288); lustrous, dark green summer foliage; white flowers in June followed by bluish, white-blotched fruits in August (289); the birds effectively strip the fruits; good plant for naturalizing or use in wet soil areas; 6 to 10' by 6 to 10'; Zone 5.

Cornus florida — Flowering Dogwood

290

291

292

293

294

295

296

297

Shrub (seldom) or small, low-branched tree with spreading horizontal lines; stratified layered effect (290, 291), usually with a flat-topped crown and often wider than high at maturity; the showy white flowers (292) occur before the leaves in May; excellent, dark green summer foliage, reddish purple in fall; alligator-like, blocky bark (293); 'Fastigiata' (294) is an upright form; 'Pluribracteata' (295) a double-flowered form; 'Pygmaea' (296) a mounded form with dark green foliage; 'Welchii' (297) a form with cream-edged leaves; one of the finest native species, excellent as a specimen, in groups, shrub border, woodland garden; requires cool, moist, acid root zone and partial shade for best growth; 20' in midwest, 20 to 40' with an equal or greater spread over the range; Zone 4 (variable).

Cornus kousa — Kousa Dogwood

298

299

300

301

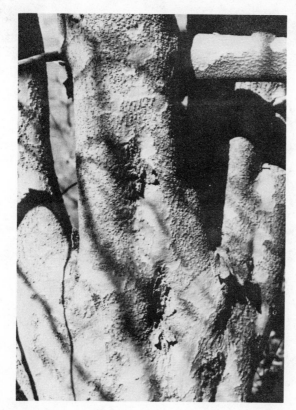

302

In youth vase-shaped; with age developing a rounded outline (298) with distinct horizontal branching habit; superior ornamental which I rate better than *C. florida*; excellent, dark green summer foliage, changing to reddish purple in fall; handsome "milky-way-like" flowers in June (299); rose-red, raspberry-shaped fruits (300) in August; bark exfoliates to create a distinct mottled appearance which is quite attractive (301, 302); specimen use is recommended; 20' high by 15 to 25' wide; Zone 5 (possibly 4).

Cornus mas — Corneliancherry Dogwood

303

305

304

Large multistemmed shrub or small tree of oval to rounded outline (303), usually branching to the ground, making successful grass culture impossible; dark green summer foliage; exfoliating, grayish to orangish brown bark (304); handsome, small yellow flowers in March; bright cherry-red fruits (305); easily cultured; nice plant for shrub border, hedge, screen and around large buildings; 20 to 25' by 15 to 20'; Zone 4.

Cornus racemosa — Gray Dogwood

306

307

Strongly multistemmed, erect-growing, suckering shrub, forming large colonies (306); grayish green foliage, changing to reddish purple in fall; very maintenance-free; tends to overstep its boundaries; white flowers in late May to early June; the white fruit (307) is relished by birds; useful in borders, masses, naturalizing; valuable in poor-soil areas; 10 to 15' by 10 to 15'; Zone 4.

Cornus sanguinea — Bloodtwig Dogwood

308

309

Often a large, unkempt, sloppily dressed, spreading, round-topped, multistemmed shrub of dense twiggy nature (308); suckering freely from the roots and forming large colonies (309), much like *C. racemosa*; dark green summer foliage; white flowers in late May to early June; black inconspicuous fruits in August; best used in masses, borders, screening; not advisable for the small property; 6 to 15' by 6 to 15'; Zone 4.

Cornus sericea — Redosier Dogwood
(formerly *C. stolonifera*)

310

311

312

Loose, broad-spreading, rounded, multistemmed shrub (310); freely stoloniferous, often forming serpentine-like branching pattern along the ground; valued (like *C. alba*) for its red winter stem color; flowers and fruits (311) are white; the cultivar 'Kelseyi' (312) is a low-growing, neat, compact form reaching 24 to 30''; species grows 7 to 9' high, spreading 10' or more; Zone 2.

Corylus americana — American Filbert or Hazelnut

313

Strongly multistemmed shrub, forming a rounded top (313) with a leggy or open base; dark green foliage, changing to orangish or reddish brown in fall; best for rough, naturalized-type areas; 10 to 15' high, spread two-thirds of, or equal to, the height; Zone 4.

Corylus avellana 'Contorta' — European Filbert or Harry Lauder's Walkingstick

314

315

A most interesting plant, offering a strong accent in the landscape (314); the leaves, and especially the stems, develop an unusual curled and twisted formation (315); 8 to 10' by 8 to 10'; Zone 4.

Corylus colurna — Turkish Filbert

316

317

Pyramidal in youth, often broadly pyramidal at maturity (316); very stately and handsome in out-line; often with a short trunk; summer foliage is a deep green; bark is brown and develops a flaky character (317); nowhere very common but tolerant of heat and cold; excellent formal outline; useful in parks, golf courses, large areas; 40 to 50' high with a spread of one-third to two-thirds the height, can grow to 70 to 80'; Zone 4.

Corylus maxima purpurea — Purple Giant Filbert

318

Similar to *C. americana* although more rounded at maturity (318); new foliage is a vivid maroon but gradually fades to dark green by July; very vigorous and colorful shrub which is best used in parks and large areas; 15 to 20' by 15 to 20'; Zone 4.

Cotinus coggygria — Common Smoketree or Smokebush

319

320

Upright, spreading, loose, open shrub (319), often wider than high at maturity (320); when heavily pruned it develops very long, slender shoots, creating a straggly unkempt appearance; summer foliage is a medium bluish green, fall color varies from yellow to red-purple; principal landscape feature is the plumose inflorescence which is predominantly evident in June-July; adapted to a wide variety of conditions; difficult to use effectively in the small landscape; 10 to 15' by 10 to 15'; Zone 4.

Cotinus obovatus — American Smoketree
(formerly *C. americanus*)

321

A large upright shrub or small tree (321); seldom grown because flowers are not as showy as *C. coggygria*, however, the leaves turn brilliant yellow-orange in fall; interesting small specimen plant for fall coloration; 20 to 30' high; Zone 5.

Cotoneaster adpressus — Creeping Cotoneaster

322

A very dwarf, close-growing, compact, rigidly branched, ground-cover-type shrub (322); leaves are a dark glossy green; rose-pink flowers in May-June; fruit bright red and vividly ornamental; cotoneasters as a group are adapted to extremes of soil and pH conditions but prefer a well-drained loam; excellent choice for groupings, masses, ground cover, foundation plantings; 1 to 1-1/2' by 4 to 6'; Zone 4.

Cotoneaster apiculatus — Cranberry Cotoneaster

323

324

Low, wide-spreading shrub with stiff, harsh-looking branching pattern; tends to mound upon itself, forming dense impenetrable tangles where leaves, bottles and paper penetrate but rakes never enter (323); dark, glossy green summer foliage with bronzy red or purplish tones in fall; rose-pink flowers in May-June; cranberry-red fruit ripening in August and effective into November; useful as a bank cover, around foundations or draped over walls; very popular in midwest and west; more coarse than *C. adpressus*; interesting when grafted on a standard (324); 3' by 3 to 6'; Zone 4.

Cotoneaster dammeri 'Skogsholmen' — Skogsholm Bearberry Cotoneaster

325

Very low-growing, semi-evergreen to evergreen, ground-cover shrub (325) with slender creeping stems which form roots in contact with the soil; lustrous, dark green foliage in summer, often assuming bronze or purple tints in winter; white flowers in May; small red fruits; another good bank or large area cover; very vigorous and has to be occasionally restrained; 1 to 1-1/2' by 6' and more; Zone 5.

Cotoneaster divaricatus — Spreading Cotoneaster

326

Spreading multistemmed shrub of rounded outline (326), outer branches long, slender, often arching, creating a fine appearance; dark, glossy green summer foliage; fluorescent, red-purple fall coloration; rose flowers in late May to early June; handsome, dark red fruit; can be successfully used in foundation plantings, groups, masses; blends well with other plants, most notably broadleaf evergreens; 5 to 6' by 6 to 8'; Zone 5.

Cotoneaster horizontalis — Rock or Rockspray Cotoneaster

327

329

328

330

A most interesting shrub which develops distinct horizontal branches (327, 328) and a fishbone branching pattern (329); the glossy, dark green leaves are deciduous in cold climates and semi-evergreen to evergreen in warmer regions; pinkish flowers and red fruits are not as effective as those of *C. apiculatus*; useful for masses, groups, ground covers; 'Tom Thumb' is a finely branched, delicate plant for rock gardens (330); 2 to 3' by 4 to 6'; Zone 5.

Cotoneaster lucidus — Hedge Cotoneaster

331

332

Erect, round-topped shrub with slender spreading branches, usually taller than broad (331); hand-some, lustrous, dark green foliage (332), changing to vivid yellow and red in fall; rose flowers and black fruits, neither of which are showy; used in hedging, screening, groups; often confused and sold as *C. acutifolius*, an inferior species; webworm can be serious; 10 to 15′ by 6 to 10′; Zone 4.

Cotoneaster multiflorus — Many-flowered Cotoneaster

333

Upright, spreading, weeping or mounded at maturity with long arching branches forming a foun-tain-like outline (333); bluish green summer foliage; beautiful white flowers; red fruit which falls soon after ripening; requires room to spread; valuable in parks, golf courses, masses, shrub borders; 8 to 12′ by 12 to 15′; Zone 4.

Crataegus crusgalli — Cockspur Hawthorn

335

334

336

Broad-rounded, low-branched tree with wide-spreading, horizontal, thorny branches which are densely set (334); the lustrous, leathery, dark green leaves often change to wine-red in fall (335); white flowers and red fruit offer multi-season interest (336); over-used by landscape designers because of horizontal features; adapted to varied soil conditions but does suffer from leaf rust; use as a single specimen, screen, or barrier; helps to soften strong vertical lines; liability in parks or high traffic areas because of thorns; var. *inermis* is a thornless form; 20 to 30' by 20 to 35'; Zone 4.

Crataegus laevigata 'Plena' — Double-flowering English Hawthorn (formerly *C. oxyacantha* 'Plena')

337

338

339

Usually a shrubby, low-branched, round-topped tree with a close dense head of stiff, zig-zag, ascending branches; the species is seldom grown; 'Plena' (337) offers double white flowers in May (338); 'Paulii' (Paul's Scarlet) (339) yields double scarlet flowers but unfortunately is often defoliated by late July; not recommended for eastern and midwestern gardens, unfortunately still widely planted; 15 to 20' by 12 to 20'; Zone 4.

Crataegus x *lavallei* — Lavalle Hawthorn

340

342

341

Dense, oval-headed, essentially thornless, small tree (340); lustrous, leathery, dark green foliage; white flowers in May; fruits are about 3/4'' in diameter and brick-red in color (341); often somewhat one-sided in outline (342); many superior hawthorns but this is still popular; 15 to 30' by 10 to 25'; Zone 4.

Crataegus mollis — Downy Hawthorn

343   344

Rounded to wide-spreading tree with varying degrees of thorniness (343); dull, medium green foliage, sporadically coloring yellowish to russet-red in fall; orangish to reddish brown bark on old trunks assumes a gnarled-spiraled condition (344); the first hawthorn to flower (white) in the mid-west; red fruit ripens in late August and falls soon thereafter; very tolerant of heavy infertile soils; quite susceptible to cedar hawthorn rust; recommended only for naturalization purposes; 20 to 30' high and as wide; Zone 4.

Crataegus monogyna 'Pygmaea' and 'Stricta' — Dwarf and Fastigiate
Singleseed Hawthorns

345   346

The species is seldom evident in cultivation; 'Stricta' (345) is a distinctly upright and narrow form (a 30-year-old plant may be 30' high and only 6 to 8' wide) and has possibility for use as a street tree and in other areas where space is limited; 'Pygmaea' (346) is a novelty item but interesting in its own small way; neither have outstanding flowers or fruits and both are ornamentally inferior to other hawthorns; Zone 4.

Crataegus nitida — Glossy Hawthorn

347

348

Dense, rounded, limitedly thorny, low-branched tree (347); extremely lustrous, dark green summer foliage; seldom seen in landscapes but quite handsome in flower (white) and fruit (dull orange-red, persisting into spring); might be worth considering over *C. laevigata*, which is very susceptible to leaf blight; bark is quite handsome (348); 25 to 30'; Zone 4.

Crataegus phaenopyrum — Washington Hawthorn

349

350

351

352

Variable; broadly columnar to somewhat rounded (349); severly thorny; new foliage reddish purple, changing to lustrous green (350) and finally red through purple in fall; white flowers in early June (the last hawthorn to flower in Illinois); excellent, small, glossy red fruits borne in great abundance and ripening in September, persistent if not ravaged by the birds (351); withstands heavy pruning (352); good specimen tree, can be used in foundation plantings around large buildings, in groupings and masses; 20 to 30' by 20 to 25'; Zone 4.

Crataegus viridis 'Winter King' — Winter King Hawthorn

354

353

355

Lovely selection with broad "V" branching structure; rounded in outline (353); very few, if any, thorns; lustrous, medium green foliage; white flowers, dull red, persistent fruit (354); young stems are a bloomy green, older branches grayish to orangish brown (355), developing a scaly constitution; excellent specimen hawthorn; perhaps the best selection available; outstanding for fruit effect and far surpasses any others mentioned above; 20 to 35' high; Zone 4.

Cryptomeria japonica — Japanese Cryptomeria

356

A pyramidal or conical evergreen tree (356) with large pom-poms of foliage, creating a poodled-type effect; needles are a bright bluish green; useful for specimen purposes; best reserved for southern midwest and east coast conditions; 50 to 60' by 20 to 30' wide; Zone 6.

Cunninghamia lanceolata — Common China-fir

357

Strongly pyramidal evergreen tree with slightly pendulous branches (357); lustrous, glaucous green summer foliage, becoming darker and bronze-tinged in cold weather; valuable as a specimen tree in the warmer parts of the country; 30 to 75'; Zone 7.

Cytisus scoparius — Scotch Broom

358

359

360

A broad, rounded-mounded shrub with very erect, slender, grass-green stems (358); stems are principal photosynthetic organ as leaves are scarce or absent (359); flowers are a glowing yellow (360); excellent in sandy, infertile, dry soils; good for stabilizing sandy right-of-ways along highways; many *Cytisus* species and cultivars, most with similar ornamental features; 5 to 6' when open-grown, twice that when used in the shrub border and in tight situations; Zone 5.

Daphne x *burkwoodii* — Burkwood Daphne

361

362

363

364

Daphnes are seldom seen in American gardens because of their fastidious cultural requirements; Burkwood Daphne is a loose irregular shrub (361); foliage bluish green; flowers white (362), often pinkish-tinged, fragrant, May; red fruits; perfers well-drained, moist near neutral (pH 6 to 7) soil, light shade; interesting plant, as are the other species, but not common; offers a distinct challenge for the adventuresome gardener; 'Somerset' (363, 364) is a densely branched, pyramidal-oval form, growing 3 to 4' high; 4 to 6'; Zone 4.

Davidia involucrata — Dove Tree

365

366

Broad pyramidal tree resembling a linden, especially in youth (365); medium green foliage (366); flowers composed of two creamy white bracts, May; will not flower every year; prefers well-drained, moist soil and partial shade; interesting plant because of unique history but a rather tempermental performer in the landscape; 20 to 40' by 20 to 40'; Zone 6.

Deutzia gracilis — Slender Deutzia

367

368

Low broad mound, graceful and free-flowering (367) with slender ascending branches; foliage flat green in summer, sometimes developing a purplish tone in fall but never very effective; excellent white flowers in May; adaptable to extremes of soil and climate; makes a good hedge, mass (368), facer or shrub border plant; often over-used because of small size; 2 to 4' by 3 to 4'; Zone 4.

Deutzia x *lemoinei* — Lemoine Deutzia

369

Very twiggy, dense, round, erect-branched shrub which requires considerable maintenance; white flowers in May are showy (369); used in masses, hedges; not a very accommodating shrub; there are many superior species; 5 to 7' by 5 to 7'; Zone 4.

Deutzia scabra — Fuzzy Deutzia

371

370

Oval or obovate, round-topped shrub, taller than broad with spreading, somewhat arching branches and often of unkempt appearance (370); flowers pure white or tinged pink outside (371), occurring ten to fourteen days after those of *D. gracilis*; a very rough-and-tumble shrub, best reserved for massing and borders; 6 to 10' by 4 to 8'; Zone 5.

Diervilla sessilifolia — Southern Bush-honeysuckle

372

Low-growing, stoloniferous shrub with arching outer branches (372), forming a broad flat mound at maturity; little-used but interesting because of glossy, dark green summer foliage and plum-purple fall color; sulfur-yellow, limitedly ornamental flowers in June; very adaptable and should be pruned in spring to keep neat; good filler, facer plant, 3 to 5' by 3 to 5' or greater; Zone 4.

Diospyros virginiana — Common Persimmon

373

374

Tree with slender, oval to rounded crown, often very symmetrical in outline (373); dark green summer foliage, changing to yellow through reddish purple in fall; interesting, yellowish to pale orange, edible fruits; bark (374) is thick, dark gray or brownish to almost black and is prominently broken into scaly squarish blocks; difficult to transplant; interesting native tree for parks, golf courses and other large areas; in southern Illinois the tree grows on coal-stripped lands and often forms thickets on dry eroding slopes and sandy soils; 35 to 60' by 20 to 35'; Zone 4.

Dirca palustris — Leatherwood

375

Under cultivation a much-branched, rather dense, oval to rounded shrub (375), in native haunts rather loose and open; light green foliage, turning yellow in fall; pale yellow flowers before the leaves in March; pale green or reddish fruit, not showy; thrives in moist, wet, shady areas; interesting shrub for naturalizing; 3 to 6' by 3 to 6'; Zone 4.

Elaeagnus angustifolia — Russian-olive

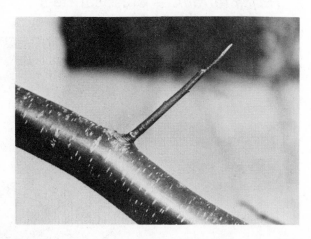

377

376

Large shrub or small tree of rounded outline (376), often quite open and of light texture; silver-gray to gray-green summer foliage; one of the best trees for gray foliage; young stems are lustrous brown, developing cherry-like lenticels (377); yellowish white, fragrant flowers in May; silver-yellow edible fruits in September; often used along highways or the seacoast because of excellent salt tolerance; susceptible to *Verticillium* wilt; 12 to 20' by 12 to 20' (can grow 30 to 40' high); Zone 2.

Enkianthus campanulatus — Redvein Enkianthus

379

378

Narrow upright shrub with layered branches and tufted foliage (378); medium green summer foliage, brilliant and unrivaled orange and red fall foliage; flowers are bell-shaped (379), whitish to yellowish and veined with red, May; requires acid soil and should be cultivated like rhododendrons; combines well with rhododendrons; superior for fall color; unfortunately, becomes somewhat open and leggy with age; 6 to 8' in cold climates but will grow larger (15' and more) in warm areas; Zone 4.

Erica tetralix — Crossleaf Heath

380

A low-growing, dainty, evergreen ground cover (380), very similar to *Calluna*; the flowers are rose-colored and open from June through September; a valuable plant for the rockery; 6 to 18''; Zone 5, less hardy than *Calluna vulgaris*.

Eucommia ulmoides — Hardy Rubber Tree

381

382

A most interesting and unusual tree of rounded to broad-rounded outline (381); extremely clean and pest-free; summer foliage is a lustrous dark green (382); very tolerant of drought and poor soil conditions; makes a valuable park, campus, estate or lawn specimen; 40 to 60' by 40 to 60'; Zone 4.

Euonymus alata — Winged Euonymus

383

384

385

386

Mounded to horizontal, spreading, flat-topped shrub (383), usually broader than high; handsome medium to dark green summer foliage and consistent, brilliant pinkish red to red fall coloration; corky winged stems (384) add an interesting element to the winter landscape; adaptable, however, does not withstand water-logged soils; essentially free from scale, which affects the other tree *Euonymus* species; valuable hedge plant (385) and often over-used for this feature; makes a good shrub-border plant and valuable in groupings; 'Compacta' (386) is densely rounded in habit with fine stems which do not develop the prominent corky wings of the species, grows to 10'; species grows 15 to 20' by 15 to 20'; Zone 3.

Euonymus bungeana — Winterberry Euonymus

387

388

389

Rounded small tree or large shrub with slender, slightly pendulous branchlets (387); light to medium green foliage holds late; the fruits (388) are pinkish and open to expose an orange-colored seed; gray-black bark (389) develops an interesting, ridged and furrowed characteristic; principal landscape problem is the tree's extreme susceptibility to scale; if kept clean, makes a nice small specimen or addition to the shrub border; 18 to 24' by 18 to 24'; Zone 4.

Euonymus europaea — European Euonymus

390

391

Usually rounded in outline (390); dull, dark green summer foliage, inconsistently yellowish to reddish purple in fall; excellent, pink to red fruit which opens to expose orange seeds (391); susceptible to scale; very handsome in fruit, especially on close inspection; 12 to 30' by 10 to 25'; Zone 3.

Euonymus fortunei — Wintercreeper Euonymus

392

393

394

395

396

397

A variable, almost indescribable species, the cultivars being of primary landscape interest; 'Coloratus' (392) is a valuable ground cover, the dark green leaves changing to plum-purple during the winter; 'Emerald Gaiety' (393) is a rounded form with pronounced white margins on the deep green leaves; 'Kewensis' (394) is a dainty prostrate type with leaves about 1/4 to 1/2'' long; 'Radicans', or var. *radicans* (395), is a variable, trailing or climbing form, often becoming quite woody; 'Vegeta' (396, 397) is a popular evergreen type of woody constitution, growing to 4', a heavy fruiter but also quite susceptible to scale; Zone 4 for all types.

Euonymus kiautschovica — Spreading Euonymus

398

399

400

Deciduous to evergreen shrub of rounded habit; good, glossy, dark green foliage; handsome fruit which opens to display orange seeds (398); culturally adaptable and not as subject to scale as the tree types; the species is not as handsome as the cultivars 'Dupont', 'Hobbs' (399), 'Manhattan', 'Newport' and 'Sieboldiana' which make excellent hedges (400), masses, groupings or foundation plants; 8 to 10' by 8 to 10'; Zone 5.

Evodia daniellii — Korean Evodia

402

401

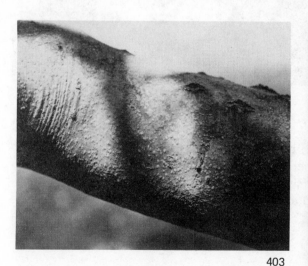

403

404

Lovely small tree of rounded to broad-rounded outline (401); lustrous, dark green, pest-resistant summer foliage; white flowers in July; reddish, two-valved, beaked fruits in August-September (402); quite adaptable to varied soil conditions; smooth, gray-brown bark (403); fine small specimen tree (404), might make a good street tree; 30 to 40' by 30 to 40'; Zone 4.

Exochorda racemosa — Common Pearlbush

406

407

405

Upright, slender-branched, loose, irregular shrub (405), becoming floppy, open and unkempt with age; often fountain-like in outline, medium green summer foliage; lovely white flowers in May (406); fruit a five-valved capsule, ripening in October and persisting (407); adaptable to varied soil conditions; best reserved for the shrub border; 9 to 15' by 10 to 15'; Zone 4.

Fagus grandifolia — American Beech

408

409

410

411

A sturdy imposing tree, often with a short trunk and oval to rounded crown (408) of bold branches (409); lustrous, dark green summer foliage and beautiful, golden brown fall coloration; E. H. Wilson, the great plant explorer, noted that "the bark is often disfigured by fledgling poets, lovers and other irresponsibles" (410); somewhat difficult to transplant, sensitive to the invasion of man; beautiful native tree (411); excellent in parks, golf courses and large areas; *unrivaled*; 50 to 70' with a maximum of 100 to 120'; Zone 3.

Fagus sylvatica — European Beech

412

413

414

415

416

417

418

419

420

Densely pyramidal-oval, branching to the ground (412) with a regular symmetry (413); a dominant plant in the landscape; leaves a tender shimmering green when unfolding, eventually lustrous dark green followed by rich brown and golden fall coloration; bark (414) develops an elephant-hide appearance as well as elephant-foot (415) configuration; culturally less demanding than *F. grandifolia*; no finer specimen tree; 'Asplenifolia' (416, 417) is graceful, cut-leaf form; 'Fastigiata' (418) is a narrow upright form; 'Pendula' (419) is a weeping form which offers interest in all seasons; 'Roseo-marginata' (420) has purple leaves with an irregular rose and pinkish white border; 50 to 60' by 35 to 45'; Zone 4.

Forsythia 'Arnold Dwarf'

421

Low-growing, broadly spreading, vigorous type (421); branches freely, rooting when in contact with the soil; flowers sparsely but makes a good ground cover; a hybrid between *F.* x *intermedia* and *F. japonica*, introduced by the Arnold Arboretum; 3' high by 6 to 8' wide; Zone 4.

Forsythia x *intermedia* cultivars — Border Forsythia

422

423

424

Upright, rank-growing, deciduous shrub, differentially developing upright and arching canes (422) which make it appear that the roots were stuck in an electric socket; medium green summer foliage; excellent yellow flowers (423) in April; will tolerate almost any conditions except those that are permanently wet; 'Karl Sax' and 'Beatrix Farrand' seem most flower-bud hardy; best used in masses (424), groups, shrub borders; 8 to 10' by 10 to 12'; Zone 4.

Forsythia suspensa — Weeping Forsythia

425

426

Upright shrub with definitely weeping, slender branches forming a fountain-like habit (425, 426); flowers (yellow) sparsely compared to *F.* x *intermedia* types; decent choice for banks, waterways, over walls where trailing branches can sweep the ground; 8 to 10' by 10 to 15'; Zone 5.

Forsythia viridissima 'Bronxensis' — Bronx Greenstem Forsythia

427

Dwarf form, growing twice as wide as tall (427); excellent bright green foliage; flowers (yellow) better than 'Arnold Dwarf'; roots easily from cuttings; excellent facer, ground cover or low mass plant; 1' by 2'; Zone 4.

Fothergilla gardenii — Dwarf Fothergilla

428

429

Small shrub with slender, crooked, often spreading branches, weakly rounded in outline (428); leathery, pest-resistant, dark green summer foliage; unrivaled, brilliant yellow to orange to scarlet fall coloration, often a combination of colors on the same leaf; honey-scented white flowers (429) in late April—early May; requires acid, peaty, moist, well-drained soils; use in foundation plantings, borders; beautiful plant; 2 to 3' by 2 to 3'; Zone 4.

Fothergilla major — Large Fothergilla

430

A pyramidal to rounded shrub, often distinctly upright-oval, of rather dense constitution (430); similar to above in foliage and flower characteristics; again, a superior plant, most deserving of a place in the garden; perhaps more tolerant of dry soils than *F. gardenii*; 6 to 10', slightly smaller in spread; Zone 4.

Franklinia alatamaha — Franklinia or Franklin Tree

431

432

433

434

Interesting small tree or large shrub of open outline (431) with foliage borne at the extremities of the branches; glossy, medium green summer foliage, rich orange-red in fall; lovely white flowers (yellow stamens) in July, August, and September (432); most interesting, capsular fruit (433); handsome, gray, fissured bark (434); requires acid, moist, well-drained soil; interesting specimen plant; 18 to 25', quite variable in spread; Zone 6, perhaps 5.

Fraxinus americana — White Ash

435

436

In youth weakly pyramidal to oval-upright; in old age developing a massive, stately, round-topped crown (435); dark green summer foliage, changing to yellow-red-maroon in fall; worthwhile shade tree, its potential has not been adequately explored; gray-brown bark (436), furrowed into close, diamond-shaped areas separated by narrow interlacing ridges; ashes as a group tolerate extremes of soil and pH but are quite susceptible to scale, cankers and borers; 50 to 80' by 50 to 80'; Zone 3.

Fraxinus angustifolia — Narrowleaf Ash

437

Upright-oval tree (437) with finer texture than *F. americana* or *F. pennsylvanica*; lustrous, dark green leaves; a good specimen tree; like many European-based ashes, its susceptibility to borers limits extensive use; 60 to 80'; Zone 5.

Fraxinus excelsior — Common or European Ash

438

Round-headed to broad-spreading outline (438); limited use because of borer susceptibility; handsome when full-grown; 70 to 80' by 60 to 90'; Zone 5.

Fraxinus holotricha 'Moraine' — Moraine Ash

439

Round-headed tree (439); good, dark green foliage; very borer-susceptible and use should be tempered; 30 to 40' by 30 to 40'; Zone 5.

Fraxinus pennsylvanica — Green Ash

440

441

Softly pyramidal in youth; developing an upright spreading outline at maturity (440) with three to five main branches and many coarse, twiggy branchlets, bending down and then up at the ends; shiny, dark green summer foliage, sporadically developing yellow fall coloration; gray-brown to black bark is furrowed into close, diamond-shaped areas separated by interlacing ridges (441); worthwhile tree for difficult areas, especially 'Marshall's Seedless'; 50 to 60', one-half to two-thirds that in spread; Zone 3.

Fraxinus quadrangulata — Blue Ash

442

443

Slender, straight, slightly tapered trunk which supports a narrow, rounded, often irregular crown of spreading branches (442); leaves are dark green in summer, changing to pale yellow in fall; bark differs from other ashes as it is broken into scaly plates (443); difficult to propagate; makes a nice specimen tree; 50 to 70' high; Zone 3.

Gaylussacia brachycera — Box Huckleberry

444

Dwarf evergreen shrub (444), spreading by underground rootstocks and forming a solid mat; dark, glossy green foliage with a reddish cast when grown in full sun; white to pink flowers in May-June; bluish fruits; requires an acid, loose, well-drained soil; lovely plant, well-suited to areas underneath pine trees and rhododendrons where the soil is acid and well-drained; 6 to 18", spreading indefinitely; Zone 5.

Genista tinctoria — Common Woadwaxen or Dyer's Greenwood

445

Low shrub with almost vertical (445), slender, green, limitedly branched stems; bright green summer foliage; yellow flowers in June with sporadic flowering on new growth thereafter; prefers hot sunny location in infertile soils which are dry, loamy or sandy; worthwhile plant for poor soils, does not perform well in heavy clay soils of midwest; 2 to 3' by 2 to 3'; Zone 2.

Ginkgo biloba — Ginkgo

447

446

448

449

Usually pyramidal in outline when young (446); in old age often becomes wide-spreading (447) with large, massive, picturesque branches (448); interesting, bright green foliage, often pure yellow fall color; extremely adaptable, seemingly thriving in urban environments; valuable park, campus, golf course, city tree; 'Fastigiata' (449) is a distinctly upright form; 50 to 80' in height with a tremendously variable spread; Zone 4.

Gleditsia triacanthos — Common Honeylocust

451

450

452

453

454

455

Open tree (450) with prominent armed thorns (451); variety *inermis* (452) develops a short trunk and rather open spreading crown of light airy composition; bright green summer foliage, fall color often a good yellow; bark (453) is broken into long, narrow, longitudinal and superficially scaly ridges; favorite plant of landscape designers (454); unfortunately, the pests have caught up with the tree, especially mimosa webworm (455); 30 to 70' by 30 to 70'; Zone 4.

Gymnocladus dioica — Kentucky Coffee Tree

456

457

458

Develops vertically ascending branches which form a narrow obovate crown (456); picturesque, ruggedly handsome, bare-limbed and somewhat clumsy-looking in winter (457); bluish green foliage, sporadically developing good yellow in fall; bark (458) a rough grayish brown with hard, thin, firm and scaly ridges, curling outward along the edges; adaptable, does particularly well in midwest; choice tree for parks, golf courses and other large areas; use male to avoid messy pods; 60 to 75' by 40 to 50'; Zone 4.

Halesia carolina — Carolina Silverbell

459

460

461

462

463

Low-branched tree with a comparatively narrow head and ascending branches (459), often with several spreading branches forming a broad-rounded crown (460); the dark green foliage (461) is extremely pest-resistant; fall color is an indifferent yellow; bark is also quite handsome (462); white bell-shaped flowers arrive with, or slightly before, the leaves in April and are exquisitely beautiful (463); lovely specimen or patio tree; 30 to 40' (80'); Zone 4.

Hamamelis japonica — Japanese Witch-hazel

464

A large shrub, often of a flattish, wide-spreading outline, with lovely, four-petaled, yellow-red flowers (464) which emerge in January and February; medium green leaves may turn yellow, orange and red in fall; seldom seen in North American gardens; 15 to 20′ and larger; Zone 5.

Hamamelis mollis — Chinese Witch-hazel

465

467

466

A large oval to rounded shrub (465); the fragrant yellow flowers appear in late January through March (466, pictured, is var. *brevipetala*); the medium green summer foliage turns to brilliant yellow in fall (467); very tough and vigorous witch-hazel that offers considerable interest to the winter landscape; highly recommended for shrub borders or possibly as a specimen plant; 20 to 25' by 20 to 25'; Zone 4.

Hamamelis vernalis — Vernal Witch-hazel

468

The smallest of the witch-hazels (468), developing into a dense, rounded, relatively neat-appearing shrub compared to *H. virginiana*; foliage is similar to that of *H. mollis* and *H. virginiana*; flowers range from yellow to almost red, emit a pungent fragrance and occur from late January through February; all witch-hazels tolerate shade well and are adapted to extremes of soil and pH conditions; works well in groups, masses, screens, barriers; not used enough in modern landscapes; 6 to 10' by 6 to 10' (can grow to 15'); Zone 5.

Hamamelis virginiana — Common Witch-hazel

469   470

Small tree or large shrub (469) with several crooked, spreading branches forming an irregular, rounded, often open crown; medium green foliage in summer, often yellow in fall, holding late and obscuring the flower effect; flowers are fragrant, usually yellow with interior of the calyx lobes brownish (470); specimens in the central Illinois area have flowered as early as mid-October and as late as early December; effective (as is true for other species) for a period of two to three weeks; fine plant for naturalizing, perhaps too coarse for a small residential landscape; 20 to 30' by 20 to 25'; Zone 4.

Hedera helix — English Ivy

471

472

473

474

Low-growing, evergreen ground cover (471) in the juvenile (non-flowering) state or a large woody vine (472, 473) when mature; mature form can be used as a broadleaf evergreen shrub under Zone 6 conditions (474); foliage is a lustrous dark green; when properly cultured (moist, acid, well-drained soil, high in organic matter, full sun or shade) this is one of the most handsome and functional evergreen ground covers; 6 to 8'' high when used as ground cover, can climb to 90' as a vine; Zone 5, though severely injured during winter of 1976-77 (−20° to −25°F), even hardy clones 'Thorndale', 'Wilson', 'Baltica' being damaged.

Hibiscus syriacus — Shrub Althea or Rose-of-Sharon

476

475

Shrub or small tree, usually erectly branched (475); summer foliage is a deep green, holding late or developing a poor yellow in fall; flowers (476) vary from white to red to purple, single or double, in solids or combinations of colors, and are borne from August into September on current season's growth; offers worthwhile late summer color but does not deserve specimen use; best in groupings, masses, shrub borders; 8 to 12' by 6 to 10'; Zone 5.

Hippophae rhamnoides — Common Seabuckthorn

477

478

Large shrub or small tree, spreading and irregularly rounded; often loose and open, suckering to form large thickets; summer foliage is a handsome silver or gray-green; fruit (477) is a bright orange-red and persists through the winter (borne only on female plants); prefers relatively infertile sandy soil; withstands salt spray; good in mass, along highways, used for stabilizing sandy areas, makes a good hedge (478); 8 to 12' (30') by 10 to 40'; Zone 3.

Hovenia dulcis — Japanese Raisin Tree

Small handsome tree of upright-oval to round outline (479) with clean ascending main branches and a paucity of lateral branches (480); glossy, medium green summer foliage; flowers not showy; fruit a light grayish or brown drupe, the infructescence a reddish color; adaptable to a wide range of conditions; nice small lawn or, perhaps, street tree; 30' by 20 to 25'; Zone 6, perhaps 5 if adequately sited.

Hydrangea anomala subsp. *petiolaris* — Climbing Hydrangea (formerly *H. petiolaris*)

483

484

485

True climbing vine, climbing by root-like holdfasts, therefore needing limited, or no, support (481, 482); develops in more than one plane and gives depth to the structure it covers; dark green, glossy summer foliage (483); rich brown bark develops an exfoliating shaggy characteristic (484); interesting, 6 to 10'' diameter, flat-topped inflorescence with sterile white flowers and fertile inner flowers (485); slow to re-establish after transplanting, with time it will proliferate in rich, well-drained, moist soil; the best vine, especially for covering large buildings; unlimited in ability to climb; extremely beautiful; Zone 4.

Hydrangea arborescens 'Grandiflora' — Hills-of-Snow Hydrangea

486

487

488

Rounded-mounded, clumpy shrub (486) with many weak, shreddy-barked, non-branched canes; dark green summer leaf color; white flowers are borne in 6 to 8″ diameter corymbs in June and remain effective for 4 to 8 weeks; prefers a shaded area where there is a cool moist root zone; best employed in the shrub border (487); 'Annabelle' (488) has extremely large corymbs (up to 1′ across); 3 to 5′ by 3 to 5′; Zone 4.

Hydrangea macrophylla — Bigleaf Hydrangea

489

Mounded-rounded shrub (489) of many erect, usually unbranched, thick stems; lustrous, medium green foliage; flowers of two types, depending on cultivar, one with sterile, showy, outer florets and fertile inner flowers, the other with predominantly sterile flowers; prefers well-drained, acid soil, the flower color of some cultivars being affected by pH (pH 5.0 to 5.5 producing blue flowers, pH 6.0 to 6.5 pink); suitable for shrub border, somewhat coarse in summer and winter; 3 to 6′ (10′), with a similar or greater spread; Zone 6.

Hydrangea paniculata 'Grandiflora' — PeeGee Hydrangea

490

Upright, coarsely spreading, small, low-branched tree or large shrub; the branches assume a semi-arching condition under the weight of the flowers (490); dark green summer foliage; flowers are white, changing to pinkish and finally brown, persistent from mid-July on; has been termed a monstrosity in the landscape; showy in flower but difficult to use in the small landscape; 15 to 25' by 10 to 20'; Zone 4.

Hydrangea quercifolia — Oakleaf Hydrangea

491

493

492

Upright, coarse, sparsely branched, irregular, stoloniferous shrub (491); good, dark green summer foliage, changing to shades of red, orangish brown and purple in fall; exfoliating, cinnamon-brown bark (492); flowers are white, changing to purplish, pink and finally brown, late June through July and August; does exceedingly well in shade; somewhat coarse in winter (493); best in masses, shrub borders; 4 to 6' by 3 to 5' and greater; Zone 5.

Hypericum calycinum — Aaronsbeard St. Johnswort

495

494

Stoloniferous, semi-evergreen shrub (494) with procumbent or ascending stems; dark green to bluish green summer foliage; bright yellow flowers on new growth in July and sporadically through September (495); does well in shady dry soil; good ground cover, as it effectively covers an area in a short time; 12 to 18'' by 18 to 24''; Zone 5, however, often killed back to ground, probably best suited to Zone 6.

Hypericum frondosum 'Sunburst' — Sunburst Golden St. Johnswort

497

496

A most beautiful cultivar of mounded habit (496); foliage is a distinct bluish green and holds late into fall; the buttercup-yellow flowers (497) occur in July; does well in dry soils, flowers on new wood so can be periodically rejuvenated; lovely facer or mass plant; 2 to 4' by 2 to 4'; Zone 5.

Hypericum patulum 'Hidcote' — Hidcote St. Johnswort

498

A compact rounded type (498) which in northern areas is often reduced to an herbaceous perennial; excellent, 2″ diameter, yellow flowers occur from late June sporadically into October; same uses as *H.f.* 'Sunburst', however, not as hardy; 18 to 24″ by 18 to 24″; Zone 6.

Hypericum prolificum — Shrubby St. Johnswort

499

Small dense shrub (499) with stout, stiff, erect stems, developing a rounded outline; handsome, bright yellow flowers in July-August; worthwhile for summer color; best in masses, groups; 2 to 4′ by 2 to 4′; Zone 4.

Ilex x *attenuata* 'Fosteri # 2' — Foster's Holly # 2

500

501

Handsome, dense, pyramidal evergreen holly (500) with lustrous, dark green foliage; very good red fruits which may persist if birds do not strip them; makes a good hedge (501) or grouping; 10 to 20' high; not particularly hardy, best reserved for Zone 6 and further south; has frozen out in central Illinois.

Ilex cornuta 'Rotunda' — Dwarf Chinese Holly
(may also go under the name *I.c.* 'Compacta' or 'Nana')

502

503

A compact, densely branched broadleaf evergreen (502) with dark, lustrous green, spinose leaves similar to those of the species; makes an excellent low hedge, mass, foundation plant or can be used in groupings; 3' by 4 to 5'; Zone 6; 'Burfordii' is a dark glossy green, its leaves terminated by a single spine; fruits are a deep red and borne in great quantities; distinctly rounded or globose in outline (503) and of dense habit; up to 10' high but can be restrained by good pruning; makes an excellent specimen, foundation, hedge, screen; a favorite landscape plant in the south; Zone 6, preferably 7.

Ilex crenata cultivars — Japanese Holly

504

505

506

507

508

509

The evergreen species is poorly defined and not used in the landscape trade, however, the following cultivars are valuable, as all have good, dark green foliage throughout the year and, if female, give rise to black fruits: 'Convexa' (504) is one of the hardiest forms (at least Zone 5), dense and wide-spreading, a 40-year-old plant being 9' by 24'; 'Helleri' (505) is a dwarf, very compact form, a 26-year-old plant being 4' by 5'; 'Hetzii' (506) is supposedly a dwarf form of 'Convexa', however, does not appear to be as hardy; 'Microphylla' (507) proves to be an upright shrub of great density, leaves are small; 'Rotundifolia' (508) is an upright rounded type, growing 8 to 12' high, the leaves 1/2 to 1'' long; 'Stokes' (509) is similar to 'Helleri' but probably not as hardy; the Japanese Hollies prefer acid, moist, well-drained soils; all make excellent hedges, foundation plants, masses and groupings; Zone 5 to 6.

Ilex decidua — Possumhaw

510

511

A large deciduous shrub with ascending branches, often slightly pendulous at the tips (510); summer foliage is a dark glossy green; fruits (511) vary from orange to scarlet and often persist through the winter; would make a good shrub border or mass planting; requires male and female for good fruit set; 7 to 15' by three-fourths that in spread, can grow to 30'; Zone 5 (4).

Ilex glabra — Inkberry

512

513

Upright, much-branched, erect-rounded evergreen shrub (512), somewhat open with age and often losing the lower leaves; lustrous, dark green foliage; fruit (on female plants) is glossy black and persistent; very tolerant of wet soils; good plant for hedges, masses, grouping; 6 to 8' by 8 to 10'; 'Compacta' (513) is a dwarf female clone, growing about half the size of the species; Zone 3.

Ilex x *meserveae* 'Blue Girl', 'Blue Boy', 'Blue Prince', 'Blue Princess', 'Blue Angel', 'Blue Maid'

514

These cultivars resulted from crosses between *I. rugosa* and *I. aquifolium*; in general, plants are shrubby bushy evergreens (514) with superior, lustrous, dark green foliage and purplish young stems; the first two mentioned cultivars have been largely discontinued; appear to be superior choices for the midwest; will grow from 6 to 15' high and as wide; possess at least Zone 5, possibly Zone 4, hardiness.

Ilex opaca — American Holly

515

516

Densely pyramidal in youth with branches to the ground, becoming in old age slightly more open, irregular and picturesque (515); evergreen foliage is a dull, usually dark green; fruits are red (516) and often persistent; best used as a specimen plant or in groupings; requires male and female for fruit set; suffers from drying winter winds, poor drainage, high-pH soils; 40 to 70' by 18 to 40', usually smaller under midwest conditions; Zone 5.

Ilex serrata — Finetooth Holly

517

Another deciduous, shrubby (517), bright-red-fruited holly, somewhat similar to *I. verticillata* in overall characteristics; 'Leucocarpa' has white fruits; 10'; Zone 5.

Ilex verticillata — Winterberry or Black-alder

518

519

Oval to rounded, deciduous shrub; deep, often lustrous green summer foliage; fruits are a lustrous red, literally cloth the branches (518) and persist into winter if not taken by the birds; very adaptable to wet soils; makes an excellent plant in the shrub border for winter color; requires male and female for fruit set; 'Winter Red' is a densely branched (519), dark-foliaged, heavily fruited type; 6 to 9' by 6 to 9', can grow larger; Zone 3.

Juglans nigra — Black Walnut

520

521

In youth an oval to rounded tree (520); at maturity developing a full, well-formed trunk which is devoid of branches a considerable distance from the ground (521); crown is oval to rounded; is not suitable for the residential landscape—too dirty, large; difficult to transplant; valued for lumber; 50 to 75′ (up to 125 to 150′); Zone 4.

Juniperus — Juniper

522

Junipers as an evergreen group exhibit great diversity of habit, foliage texture and color (522). Very few juniper species are used in landscaping, and the emphasis has been placed on cultivars. The following descriptions emphasize the cultivars, in most cases, rather than the species. Junipers withstand extremes of soils and temperatures, making them favorite landscape plants in the midwest and plains states.

Juniperus chinensis — Chinese Juniper (Zone 4)

523

524

525

526

'Hetzii' — Large, rapidly growing, upright-spreading form; will take pruning quite well (523); needles bluish green, scale-like and awl-shaped; produces numerous, fleshy grayish green cones; 10 to 15' by 10 to 15', usually smaller.

'Keteleeri' — Broad-pyramidal tree with a stiff trunk and loose, light to medium green, scale-like foliage (524); bears great numbers of grayish green, berry-like cones; makes an excellent screen or privacy barrier (525); 20 to 30'.

'Old Gold' — Quite similar to 'Pfitzer', only more compact (526) with yellow new growth during summer, changing to bronze-gold during winter; 3 to 5' by 5 to 7.5'.

527

528

529

530

'Pfitzeriana' - The granddaddy of juniper cultivars; foliage is a medium green color; probably the most widely planted juniper; makes a good container plant (528); wide-spreading form usually listed as growing 5' by 10' but actually can grow two to three times that size (527).

'Pfitzeriana Aurea' — Similar to 'Pfitzer' in growth; branchlets and leaves tinged golden yellow in summer, changing to yellowish green in winter (529).

'Pfitzeriana Compacta' — Bushy, compact, low-growing form (530); superior because of smaller size and neater habit.

'Pyramidalis' — A rather poor juniper; pyramidal-columnar, dense with ascending branches (531); leaves needle-like, bluish green; often exhibiting bare spots and dead areas; 10 to 15'.

'Robusta Green' — Distinct upright form with tufted, brilliant green foliage (532).

'San Jose' — Low-growing type, spreading irregularly (533); foliage grayish green, mostly acicular; susceptible to juniper blight; 12 to 15'' by 6 to 8'.

var. *sargentii* — One of the best!; blue-green, scale-like foliage; one of the most functional junipers available (534); salt-tolerant and blight-resistant; low-growing (18'' to 2' high), wide-spreading (7.5 to 9') (535).

Juniperus communis — Common Juniper

536

537

538

539

Variable, sprawling, spreading shrub or medium-sized, small tree with ascending branches; old pastures (536) are often overgrown with Common Juniper, and the variation in the plants is evident; Zone 2.

'Depressa Aurea' — Dwarf prostrate shrub (537); yellow foliage which in winter turns a depressing yellow-brown; rarely above 2 to 3'.

'Hibernica' ('Stricta') — In youth dense, upright; with age becoming loose, open, unkept and unattractive (538); bluish green, awl-shaped foliage; 10 to 20'.

'Suecica' — Similar to above (539), except the tips of the branchlets droop; leaves bluish green; about as lousy as above.

Juniperus conferta — Shore Juniper

540

541

Dense, bushy, procumbent shrub (540, 541), forming large evergreen mats of bright, bluish green foliage; especially well-adapted for planting in sandy soil; extremely salt-tolerant; one of the best ground cover junipers for southern midwest, east and south; 12 to 18″ by 6 to 9′; not reliably hardy in Zone 5, although it performs well in protected places.

542

'Blue Pacific' — Does not grow as large as the species; tends towards a trailing habit (542); very handsome plant with ocean-colored, blue-green foliage.

Juniperus horizontalis — Creeping Juniper

543

544

545

546

547

Numerous interesting selections have been made—the following represent a smattering of the most popular and best; species varies from 1 to 2' by 4 to 8'; Zone 3.

'Bar Harbor' — Excellent, low-growing, spreading form (543, 544); needles chiefly awl-shaped, loosely appressed, bluish green, turning plum-purple in winter; 1' by 6 to 8'.

'Blue Chip' — Low prostrate form (545) with excellent, bluish green foliage through the winter; 8 to 10'' high.

'Blue Rug' ('Wiltoni') — Very flat-growing form (546, 547) with trailing branches; intense, silvery blue foliage, assuming a slight purplish tinge in winter; fairly fast-growing; 4 to 6'' by 6 to 8'.

548

549

550

551

552

553

'Douglasi' ('Waukegan') — Trailing form (548); good, bluish green summer foliage, turning purplish in winter; rapid-growing; very functional evergreen for banks where grass maintenance is difficult; 1 to 1-1/2' by 6 to 9'.

'Plumosa' ('Andorra') — Wide-spreading, dense, compact form (549, 550); leaves awl-shaped and scale-like; somewhat plume-like in texture; bluish green in summer, changing to plum-purple in winter; quite susceptible to juniper blight; 2' by 10'.

'Plumosa Compacta Youngstown' — Compact form of 'Plumosa' which supposedly does not turn plum-purple in cold weather (551), however, various plants I have seen did assume a purplish tinge.

'Turquoise Spreader' — Low-growing, wide-spreading form (552); densely covered with soft feathery branchlets of turquoise-green foliage; vigorous grower; lovely plant; 6 to 10'' by 6 to 10'.

'Webberi' — Another low, mat-like, spreading form of fine texture (553); bluish green foliage; good-looking plant.

Juniperus procumbens — Japgarden Juniper
(*J. chinensis* var. *procumbens* according to *Hortus III*)

554

555

A dwarf, procumbent, wide-spreading, stiffly branched, blue-green-foliaged, ground-cover-type juniper (554); like all junipers, requires full sun; thrives on high-pH soils; susceptible to juniper blight; 12 to 24'' by 10 to 15'; Zone 4.

'Nana' — Dwarf bunchy grower (555), forms a compact mat with branches one on top of the other; bluish green foliage, slightly purplish in winter; 1' by 4 to 5'.

Juniperus sabina — Savin Juniper

556

557

Inadequately described in the literature; as I have observed it, either a spreading shrub, somewhat vase-shaped with stiff branches borne at a 45° angle (556), or a tightly branched, ascending small tree (557); Zone 4.

558

559

560

561

'Arcadia' — Similar in habit to var. *tamariscifolia* but lower (558, 559); grass-green, predominantly scale-like foliage; resistant to juniper blight; 1' by 4'.

'Skandia' — Similar to 'Arcadia' but slightly larger (560); foliage mostly acicular, pale grayish green; resistant to juniper blight.

var. *tamariscifolia* — Low, spreading, mounded form (561); branches horizontal, branchlets crowded; leaves awl-shaped, very short, nearly appressed, bluish green; although listed as susceptible to juniper blight, this variety has shown good resistance in the midwest; 18" by 10 to 15' in 15 to 20 years.

Juniperus scopulorum — Rocky Mountain Juniper

Usually a narrow pyramidal tree with strongly ascending branches; seldom used in the midwest and eastern states; susceptible to cedar apple rust (alternate host); 30 to 40' by 3 to 15'; Zone 4.

562

563

564

'Blue Heaven' ('Blue Haven') — Neat pyramidal form (562); foliage strikingly blue in all seasons; 20' in 15 to 20 years.

'Skyrocket' — Almost candle-like in habit; uniquely columnar; somewhat of a novelty (563); bluish green foliage.

'Springbank' — Good-looking, handsome, blue-foliaged form (564); somewhat wider-spreading than other *J. scopulorum* clones.

Juniperus squamata 'Meyeri' — Meyer's Singleseed Juniper

565

566

Bushy dense form (565) when young; somewhat open, especially at base, at maturity (566); striking bluish white, needle-like foliage; exotic-looking when young, but the dead needles persist and, after a time, the plant becomes a liability; 6 to 8' by 4 to 6'; Zone 4.

Juniperus virginiana — Eastern Redcedar

567

568

Dense pyramid in youth, maintaining a rather full complement of foliage in old age (567); medium green summer foliage, becoming dirty green in winter; bark (568) is reddish brown, exfoliating in wide strips; 40 to 50' by 8 to 20'; Zone 2.

569

'Canaertii' — Compact pyramidal form (569); dark green leaves, on young branchlets scale-like, on old ones awl-shaped; foliage tufted at ends of branches; quite susceptible to cedar apple rust; 20' in 15 years.

Kalmia angustifolia — Lambkill Kalmia

570

Low-growing evergreen shrub (570) with two forms, one a compact tufted grower, the other thin and open; flowers are a rosy purple, June or July; best for naturalizing and most certainly not as beautiful as *K. latifolia*; 1 to 3' high and wide; Zone 2.

Kalmia latifolia — Mountain-laurel

571

572

573

574

Large robust evergreen shrub which, if not crowded, is symmetrical and dense in youth (571); in old age becomes open, straggly, loose, with picturesquely gnarled trunks and limbs; glossy, dark green foliage; beautiful flowers, especially the buds, which open to pink or white in June (572, 573); requires acid, organic, well-drained soils and cool summer temperatures; does not perform well in midwest; makes a splendid mass (574), especially in shady situations; a most beautiful broadleaf evergreen; 7 to 15' (to 30') by 7 to 15'; Zone 4.

Kalopanax pictus — Castor-aralia

575

576

In youth upright-oval to obovate (575); in old age assuming an open rounded appearance with massive heavy branches; dark glossy green, almost tropical-looking summer foliage; white flowers, July-August; black fruit; requires deep, moist, rich soil for best growth; a most unusual tree for northern areas; possibly a specimen plant but very difficult to blend with other plants because of unusual texture; stems are armed with large, broad-based prickles (576); may reach 40 to 60' under cultivation; Zone 4.

Kerria japonica — Japanese Kerria

577

578

579

Upright-arching stems, forming a low, broad, dense, twiggy mass (577, 578); bright green summer foliage; interesting, yellowish green winter stem color; bright yellow flowers in April-May and sporadically thereafter (579); prefers well-drained soil; most interesting, free-flowering shrub, of worth in masses, the shrub border, as facer plant; 3 to 6' by 6 to 9'; Zone 4.

Koelreutaria paniculata — Panicled Goldenrain Tree

580

581

582

583

584

585

586

Beautiful, densely foliaged tree of regular rounded outline (580), sparingly branched, the branches spreading and ascending (581); foliage (582) is purplish red when unfolding, rich green in summer; bark is a rich brown with prominent orangish lenticels (583), developing ridged and furrowed character at maturity (584); flowers are bright yellow, July, and extremely showy; fruit is a papery, three-valved capsule (585); withstands drought, heat, wind and alkaline soils; choice specimen or valuable in groupings (586); 30 to 40' by 30 to 40'; Zone 5.

Kolkwitzia amabilis — Beautybush

588

587

Upright-arching, deciduous, vase-shaped shrub, somewhat fountain-like in overall effect; dull green summer foliage; flowers are pink with a yellow throat, late May-June and literally cover the entire plant (587); of easy culture, withstands pruning and will make a respectable hedge (588), however, the flower effect is lost; best used in the shrub border; 6 to 10′ high and larger; Zone 4.

Laburnum x *watereri* — Waterer Laburnum

589

590

Distinctly upright-oval to obovate small tree or large shrub of rather gaunt proportions (589), often leggy at base; bright, almost bluish green summer foliage; flowers (590) are bright yellow and borne in 6 to 10″ long, pendulous panicles in mid to late May; very intriguing when in flower; adapted to varied soil conditions but appears to suffer from a stem blight or canker problem; best in shrub border or where the base of the plant is screened by low-growing shrubs; 12 to 15′ by 9 to 12′; Zone 5.

Lagerstroemia indica — Crapemyrtle

591

593

592

Small tree (591) or large shrub (592) of variable habit; often seen in multistemmed form with a cloud of foliage reserved to the upper one-third of the plant, while the basal portion is leafless and only the handsome bark is evident; emerging leaves are bronze, turning medium to dark green at maturity, fall color ranges from yellow-orange to red, usually with all colors interspersed on the same tree; bark (593) is smooth, gray, exfoliating, exposing vari-colored underbark which ranges from gray through rich brown; pink to deep red flowers on 6 to 8″ long by 3 to 5″ wide panicles, July through September; prefers moist, well-drained soils, full sun; handsome and beautiful specimen shrub or tree; used extensively in south for every imaginable purpose; 15 to 25′ high with variable spread; Zone 7.

Larix decidua — European Larch

594

595

596

597

A deciduous conifer, pyramidal with horizontal branches and drooping branchlets (594); slender and supple in youth but often irregular in old age (595); bright to deep green needle color in summer, ochre-yellow in fall; cones are interesting (596) and persistent; makes a nice specimen for parks and large areas; 'Pendula' is an unusual form with extremely pendulous branchlets (597), can be grafted high or used almost as a ground cover; 70 to 75' and one-half as wide; Zone 2.

Lespedeza bicolor — Shrub Bushclover

598

Upright, somewhat open, loosely branched shrub (598) of rather delicate proportions; clover-green summer foliage; rosy purple flowers on new growth in July; requires light, sandy, well-drained soil; often dies back in severe winters and is best treated as an herbaceous perennial in northern areas; 6 to 9' and slightly less in spread; Zone 4.

Leucothoe axillaris — Coast Leucothoe

599

Similar to *L. fontanesiana* in most respects (599), except greater resistance to leaf spot disease which is so troublesome on *L. fontanesiana*; 2 to 4' (6') by one and one-half times that in spread; Zone 6(5).

Leucothoe fontanesiana — Drooping Leucothoe
(formerly *L. catesbaei*)

600

601

602

Very graceful, broadleaf evergreen shrub with long, spreading, arching branches, creating a fountain-like outline (600); new growth bright green or bronze, changing to lustrous dark green and developing a plum-purple winter coloration; fragrant white flowers are borne in axillary racemes (601) in May; prefers shade and acid, well-drained, moist soil; very intolerant of windy, droughty conditions; 'Nana' (602) is a compact form about 2' by 6'; best used in shady areas, on banks, in masses and borders; 3 to 6' by 3 to 5'; Zone 4.

Ligustrum amurense — Amur Privet

603

604

Dense, upright, multistemmed deciduous shrub of pyramidal-rounded outline (603); flat, medium to dark green summer foliage; white, sickeningly fragrant flowers in June; black fruits; of easy culture, as is true for all privets; used extensively for hedges (604), but there are superior plants; most people have never seen the flowers or fruits of privet since the buds are usually pruned off; 12 to 15', two-thirds to equal that in spread; Zone 3.

Ligustrum obtusifolium — Border Privet

605

606

607

Multistemmed deciduous shrub of broad horizontal outline (605), broadest at the top; medium to dark green summer foliage, sometimes russet to purplish in fall; white flowers; black fruit; possibly the best privet because of interesting growth habit; makes a good hedge (606), screen, barrier; variety *regelianum* (607) is lower growing (4 to 5'); 10 to 12' by 12 to 15'; Zone 3.

Ligustrum x *vicaryi* — Golden Vicary Privet

608

A dense, haystack to rounded deciduous shrub (608) with yellow foliage throughout the growing season, especially when located in full sun; widely used for color accent in the landscape; at times almost gaudy; result of cross between *L. ovalifolium* 'Aureum' and *L. vulgare*; 6 to 8' high; Zone 4.

Ligustrum vulgare — Common or European Privet

609

610

611

Stout, much-branched deciduous shrub with irregularly spreading branches (609); foliage is a dark green; white flowers (610); fruits a lustrous black (611); has lost considerable favor and been supplanted by *L. amurense* and *L. obtusifolium* in northern areas; seriously susceptible to mildew and anthracnose twig blight; 12 to 15' by 12 to 15'; Zone 4

Lindera benzoin — Spicebush

612

613

Rounded shrub of loose outline (612), much more dense when open-grown than in native situations; dark green summer foliage, sporadically yellowish in the fall; interesting yellowish green flowers in April; scarlet fruits (613) on female plants in September; prefers moist, well-drained soils; excellent in shady areas, shrub borders or naturalized situations; 6 to 12' by 6 to 12'; Zone 4.

Liquidambar styraciflua — Sweetgum

614

615

616

617

618

Decidedly pyramidal when young (614), of very uniform outline, developing a pyramidal-oval to rounded crown at maturity (615, 616); summer foliage a deep glossy green, developing rich, yellow-purple-red tones in fall; gray-brown bark (617) is deeply furrowed with narrow, somewhat rounded ridges; best growth occurs in moist, acid, well-drained soils; excellent lawn, park or street tree; 'Gumball' (618) is a cute, diminutive, multistemmed, globose form; 60 to 75' with a spread of two-thirds to equal the height; Zone 5.

Liriodendron tulipifera — Tulip Tree, **also called** Tulip Poplar, Yellow Poplar

619

620

621

622

Weakly pyramidal in youth (619), often massive in old age (620); bright, glossy green summer foliage, turning golden-yellow to yellow in fall; brownish, ridged and furrowed bark (621); interesting, tulip-shaped (622), green-yellow-orange flowers in May; prefers moist, deep, well-drained, acid soils; drought induces leaf scorch and premature defoliation; best in large areas, unfortunately is often used on streets, small properties, other restricted growing areas; *needs room*; 70 to 90' by 35 to 60' (potential to 180'); Zone 5.

Lonicera alpigena — Alps Honeysuckle

623

624

An erect, much-branched shrub (623), eventually developing a rounded outline; leaves are lustrous, dark green and offer perhaps the finest foliage among the cultivated honeysuckles; flowers are yellow-green, tinged with dull red, May; fruits are red, cherry-like, up to 1/2'' long; worthwhile honeysuckle for screens, hedges, groupings; 'Nana' (624) is a dwarf form, growing about 3' high; 4 to 8' and as wide; Zone 4.

Lonicera x bella — Belle Honeysuckle

625

Large, coarse, loosely branched shrub of mounded proportions (625); bluish green foliage; pinkish flowers which fade to yellow-white in May; red fruit; like all honeysuckles, extremely well-adapted to varied soils and climates; very functional plant for less than ideal conditions; extremely vigorous shrub of use in screening; not recommended for the small garden; 10 to 15' and one and one-half times that in spread; Zone 4 (3).

Lonicera fragrantissima — Winter Honeysuckle

626

627

Wide-spreading, irregularly branched shrub, forming a tough impenetrable thicket of stems (626, 627); dark, bluish or grayish green summer foliage, holding late into fall; flowers creamy white, lemon-scented and extremely fragrant, though not very showy, before the leaves in late March-early April; very adaptable shrub; good hedge, often used in massing, along highways and in other poor soil areas; 6 to 10' (15') by 6 to 10'; Zone 4.

Lonicera x *heckrottii* — Everblooming or Goldflame Honeysuckle

628

A vine of unknown origin; great vigor; bluish green summer foliage; flowers are yellow-pink-red, June, and continue through summer; very prolific flowering vine (628) and often used to cover unsightly structures, rock piles, fences; 10 to 15' and greater; Zone 4.

Lonicera japonica — Japanese Honeysuckle

629

630

Weedy, twining, semi-evergreen vine (629) (evergreen in south); dark green summer color; white flowers turning yellowish (630), extremely fragrant, June-September; black fruits; almost a liability but will tolerate the poorest of soils; worthwhile for covering banks, slopes, poor-soil areas; can grow 15 to 30'; Zone 4.

Lonicera maackii — Amur Honeysuckle

631

632

633

Large, upright-spreading, leggy shrub (631); medium green summer foliage; white flowers, changing to yellow, in early June; good red fruit (632) in October which offers a substantial staple for birds; very large and coarse honeysuckle (633); perhaps should be reserved for the shrub border; 12 to 15' by 12 to 15'; Zone 2.

Lonicera morrowi — Morrow Honeysuckle

634

A broad, rounded; dense, tangled mound (634) with branches and foliage to the ground; grayish to bluish green foliage; creamy white flowers, changing to yellow, May; fruit is a blood-red berry but usually not effective; acceptable for hedge use, massing, along highways and other impossible sites; 6 to 8' by 6 to 10'; Zone 4 (3).

Lonicera sempervirens — Trumpet Honeysuckle

636

635

A twining vine without the bold vigor of *L. japonica* (635) and capable of covering structures without overrunning them; bluish green summer foliage; red flowers (636) from June through August; bright red fruit; makes a good cover on porches, trellises, fences, in poor soils; 10 to 20'; Zone 3.

Lonicera tatarica — Tatarian Honeysuckle

637

638

One of the most popular honeysuckles; upright, strongly multistemmed, the branches often arching to form a rounded outline (637); bluish green summer foliage; pink to white flowers in May; red fruit (638) in July-August; makes a good barrier, hedge, screen; many worthwhile cultivars; 10 to 12' by 10'; Zone 3.

Lonicera xylosteum — European Fly Honeysuckle

639

640

Rounded mound with spreading arching branches (639); gray-green foliage; flowers white; fruits dark red; seldom employed in modern landscapes; 'Emerald Mound' (640) is a superior, low-growing (3 to 5'), mounded form with rich, emerald green foliage; 8 to 10' by 10 to 12'; Zone 4.

Maackia amurensis — Amur Maackia

641

642

Small, round-headed tree (641), quite dapper in outline when properly grown; medium to dark green summer foliage; bark is a rich shining brown, peeling with maturity and developing a curly consistency (642); flowers dull white, July and August; prefers good, loose, well-drained, acid or alkaline soil; would make a nice specimen or perhaps street tree; 20 to 30' (45') by 20 to 30'; Zone 5.

Maclura pomifera — Osage-orange or Hedge-apple

643

644

645

Develops a short trunk and low, rounded, irregular crown composed of stiff, spiny, interlacing branches (643, 644); lustrous, bright green foliage, often a good clear yellow in fall; bark (645) ashy brown or dark orange-brown with irregular longitudinal fissures and scaly ridges; very tough tree, tolerates poor soil and could prove valuable under polluted city conditions; 20 to 40' (and larger) with a comparable spread; Zone 4.

Magnolia acuminata — Cucumbertree Magnolia

647

646

648

649

Pyramidal (646) in youth (20 to 30 years); in old age developing a rounded outline with massive (647), wide-spreading branches; dark green summer foliage; interesting gray-brown bark (648); yellow-green flowers (649) in May through early June; pinkish red, cucumber-shaped fruits; magnolias as a group do not tolerate extremes of soils, preferring those that are loamy, deep, moist, well-drained, and slightly acid; should be transplanted in the spring; handsome tree for large properties, parks, golf courses; not well-known but could be effectively utilized; 50 to 80' by 50 to 80'; Zone 4.

Magnolia grandiflora — Southern Magnolia

650

651

652

653

Densely pyramidal, low-branching, stately evergreen tree (650); beautiful, lustrous, dark green leaves (651); large, fragrant, 8 to 12'' diameter, creamy white flowers (652) in June and sporadically thereafter; bark (653) develops a slight shaggy character; most definitely a specimen tree; 60 to 80' by 30 to 50'; reserved for Zone 6 conditions and areas where winter winds are minimal.

Magnolia heptapeta — Yulan Magnolia
(formerly *M. denudata*)

655

654

Small, upright-oval to rounded tree (654), usually low-branched; dark green summer foliage; white, fragrant, 4 to 6'' diameter flowers in April before the leaves (655); responds to early warm weather, and upon opening the flowers are often killed by late freezes; one of the parents of *M.* x *soulangiana*; doubtfully preferable to the hybrid species; 30 to 40'; Zone 5.

Magnolia kobus — Kobus Magnolia

656

Densely pyramidal, low-branched tree of uniform outline (656); dark green summer foliage; white flowers in April, not as large or profusely borne as those of other species; requires many years when grown from seed to develop full flowering potential; 30 to 50' by 20 to 35'; Zone 4.

Magnolia x *loebneri* — Loebner Magnolia

657

658

A dense, rounded to broad-rounded tree (657); dark green summer foliage; white, twelve-petaled, fragrant flowers (658) in mid to late April; a hybrid species (*M. stellata* x *M. kobus*); 'Merrill', a prolific-flowering, vigorous type, is available in the trade; good specimen plant; 20 to 30' by 20 to 40'; Zone 5.

Magnolia macrophylla — Bigleaf Magnolia

659

660

Pyramidal to round-headed, cumbersome giant (659) of extremely coarse texture; dark green leaves up to 32" long; creamy white, 8 to 10" across (sometimes 14" across), fragrant flowers (660) in June; difficult to use effectively because of coarseness; 30 to 40'; Zone 5.

Magnolia quinquepeta — Lily Magnolia
(formerly *M. liliflora*)

661

662

Rounded shrubby magnolia of rather uniform proportions (661); dark green summer foliage; red-purple flowers (662) occur in late April or early May just as leaves emerge; makes a lovely shrubby magnolia for borders or restricted areas; 8 to 12' by 8 to 12'; Zone 5.

Magnolia x *soulangiana* — Saucer Magnolia

663

664

665

666

Large spreading shrub or small, low-branched tree, forming a rounded outline (663); dark green summer foliage; lovely, white-pink-purplish flowers in April before the leaves (664); flowers can be injured by late spring frosts; the artistic branching habit (665) and gray bark (666) offer pleasing winter characteristics; nice specimen tree and often overused for this purpose; 20 to 30', usually with a variable spread; Zone 5.

Magnolia stellata — Star Magnolia

667

668

669

670

Dense shrub or small tree, usually of thick constitution from the close-set leaves and stems (667, 668); dark green summer foliage, often turning yellow to bronze in fall; pink to white, double, fragrant, 3″ diameter flowers (669, 670) in April; often injured by late frosts; nice single specimen or accent plant; very popular magnolia, with ample justification; 15 to 20′ by 10 to 15′; Zone 4.

Magnolia tripetala — Umbrella Magnolia

671

672

673

Similar to *M. macrophylla*, possibly more pyramidal-oval in outline (671); large (24''), dark green leaves; solitary, 6 to 10'' diameter, creamy white, unpleasantly scented flowers (672) in late May-early June; pinkish-red fruit (as is true for all magnolias) is a large aggregate of follicles (673); leaves clustered near ends of branches, creating an "umbrella-like" effect; too coarse for most landscapes but of worth to the enthusiast; 15 to 30' (40'); Zone 5.

Magnolia virginiana — Sweetbay Magnolia

674

675

676

677

Small multistemmed shrub of loose, open, upright-spreading habit in the north (674), more tree-like in the south (675); dark, glossy green foliage, holding late into fall; creamy white, lemon-scented flowers in June (676) and sporadically thereafter; handsome red fruit in August-September (677); extremely susceptible to chlorosis, more so than any other magnolia; nice specimen, patio tree; interesting effects created in wind when the silvery undersides of the leaves are exposed; 10 to 20' by 10 to 20' in the north, can grow to 60' in the south; Zone 5, preferably 6.

Mahonia aquifolium — Oregon Grapeholly

678

680

679

681

Limitedly branching evergreen shrub with upright heavy stems, often stoloniferous in habit; actually, there are two forms, one low, broad, dense and rounded (678), the other taller with upright branches, irregular and open (679); reddish bronze foliage when unfolding, lustrous dark green in summer (680), bronzed to purplish in fall and winter; bright yellow flowers (681) in April, followed by waxy blue berries in September; prefers acid, moist soils high in organic matter and shelter from drying winter winds; use as a foundation plant, in the shrub border or in masses, good in shady areas; 3 to 6' (9'), spread indefinite; Zone 4, preferably 5.

Mahonia bealei — Leatherleaf Mahonia

Clumsy, upright, coarse evergreen shrub (682); dull, dark, blue-green foliage; lemon-yellow, fragrant flowers in April; waxy blue fruit (683) ripening in August-September; used prolifically in southern areas; interesting flowers and fruits; coarse landscape shrub; 10 to 12'; Zone 6.

Mahonia repens — Creeping Mahonia

Low, stoloniferous, evergreen ground cover of stiff habit (684); lustrous, dark green summer foliage, plum-purple winter color; deep yellow flowers; blackish fruits, covered with a blue bloom; makes an unusual ground cover because of multi-season qualities; 10 to 12'', spreading indefinitely, but slowly, in good soil; Zone 4.

Malus — Flowering Crabapple

685

686

687

This is a most charming, worthwhile and misunderstood group of landscape trees, offering excellent flower, fruit and winter habit. Crabapples are available for every landscape and can be fashioned to fit into those where space is limited. They can be trained (685) or grouped (686) to create interesting effects. Branching and bark offer worthwhile winter qualities (687). The following crabapples represent just a smattering of those available. Crabapples prefer moist, well-drained, acid soil for best growth. Most are hardy in Zone 4.

Malus x *atrosanguinea* — Carmine Crabapple

688

Low-branched, rounded-mounded tree (688); good rose-pink flowers in May; dark red, sparsely produced fruits; one of the better small crabapples; very resistant to scab, variable resistance to fireblight; 15' by 15 to 20'.

Malus 'Coralburst'

689

Small, dainty, dwarf type, forming a rounded bushy head (689); double, rose-pink flowers; resistant to scab, mildew and fire blight; 8'.

Malus coronaria and *M. ioensis* — Wild Sweet and Prairie Crabapples

690

Two genetically distinct crabapples, however, very similar from a landscape aspect; usually wide-spreading, low-branched, hawthorn-like habit (690); single, white to pinkish, fragrant flowers in late May; green fruit; very susceptible to cedar apple rust; not recommended, but many cultivars of the two species are planted; 20 to 30'.

Malus floribunda — Japanese Flowering Crabapple

691

692

693

694

695

696

Over the years this species has served as the standard by which all others were judged; broad-spreading (691), architecturally perfect tree with lovely trunk and branch structure (692, 693); deep red buds (694) give rise to fragrant, pink to white flowers (695) in May; yellow to brown to red fruit (696); slightly susceptible to scab and mildew, moderately susceptible to fireblight; one of the best crabapples; 15 to 25' by 20' to 30'.

Malus 'Hopa'

697

698

One of the worst, but most widely planted, crabapples; forming a dense rounded crown (697); often develops water sprouts (698); flowers rose-pink when fully open; dull red-maroon fruit; admittedly spectacular in flower, however, tremendously susceptible to apple scab and may be defoliated by July if the spring is rainy; 20 to 25'.

Malus hupehensis — Tea Crabapple

699

700

Vase-shaped (699), decidedly picturesque outline; white flowers in May; greenish yellow to red fruit; susceptible to fireblight; one of the most handsome crabapples for form (700); 20 to 25'.

Malus 'Mary Potter'

701

Low-growing, wide-spreading form of rather loose branch structure (701); good white flowers in May; red fruit; cross between *M. sargentii* and *M.* x *atrosanguinea*; slightly susceptible to scab, mildew and fireblight; 8 to 12' by one and one-half that in width.

Malus 'Oekonomierat Echtemeyer' or 'Pink Weeper'

702

Weeping mounded form, at times somewhat mop-like (702); purplish pink flowers; purplish red fruit; extremely susceptible to apple scab; interesting for weeping habit; 10 to 15'.

Malus x *purpurea* 'Lemoine'

703

Large dense, rounded form (703); leaves purplish when unfolding, finally dark green; purple-red to crimson flowers; purplish red fruit; highly resistant to scab and fireblight; 25 to 30'.

Malus 'Red Jade'

704

Gracefully weeping form of mounded outline (704); white flowers; glossy red fruit; moderately susceptible to scab and mildew; possibly the best of the weeping types; 15'.

Malus sargentii — Sargent Crabapple

705

Mounded, densely branching, wide-spreading form (705); white flowers; dark red fruits; slightly susceptible to scab, fireblight and leaf spot; an excellent small crabapple; 6 to 10' high, one and one-half that in spread.

Malus 'Snowdrift'

706

Rounded, dense, good vigorous grower, proving to be a superior cultivar (706); white flowers; orange-red fruits; slight susceptibility to scab and fireblight; 15 to 25'.

Malus 'White Angel'

707

Tends towards a rounded outline (707); pure white flowers; large, 3/4 to 1'' diameter, glossy red fruit; slightly susceptible to cedar apple rust; flowers and fruits so heavily that vegetative growth is often reduced; 20 to 25'.

Malus x *zumi* 'Calocarpa'
(formerly *M. sieboldii zumi* 'Calocarpa')

708

709

710

Pyramidal to rounded, densely branched form of regular proportions; spectacular in flower (708), pink or red in bud, opening white to pinkish white (709); bright red fruits (710); slightly susceptible to scab, mildew, and severely so to fireblight; very popular and lovely crabapple; 25'.

Menispermum canadense — Common Moonseed

711

Deciduous twining vine with slender stems, requiring support; large, dark green leaves (711) in summer; very coarse-textured vine in all seasons; adaptable, tolerates poor soil; possibly used for screening unsightly areas, unfortunately, it also needs screening; almost a weed; 10 to 15'; Zone 4.

Metasequoia glyptostroboides — Dawn Redwood

712

713

Dense, pyramidal, deciduous conifer (712, 713), usually maintaining a central leader; bright green summer foliage, changing to rich brown in fall; orangish to reddish brown bark; makes a good specimen plant or can be used effectively in groupings; 50 to 75′ (100′) by 25 to 35′; Zone 4.

Morus alba — White or Common Mulberry

714

715

716

717

Extremely dense, round-topped tree with a profusion of tight-knit, slender branches; often develops a witches' broom which gives the tree a messy unkempt appearance (714); lustrous, dark green summer foliage; purplish black fruit (715); of little value for the modern landscape because of messiness; definitely a weedy species but tolerant of drought and polluted areas; 'Pendula' is a weeping fruiting form (716, 717) which offers unusual architecture; 30 to 50' by 30 to 50'; Zone 4.

Myrica pensylvanica — Northern Bayberry

718

719

720

Deciduous to semi-evergreen, upright-rounded, densely foliaged shrub (718); spreading and suckering in loose soil to form large colonies (719); lustrous, dark green and disease-free foliage; handsome bluish gray fruits (720) on female plants persist through the winter; develops chlorosis in high-pH soils, best in loose acid soils; use in masses, borders, poor-soil areas along highways; very salt-tolerant; 5 to 12' by 5 to 12'; Zone 2.

Nyssa sylvatica — Black Tupelo, Black Gum, Sour Gum, or Pepperidge

721

722

723

One of our most beautiful native trees; softly pyramidal when young with densely set branches (721), some of which are pendulous; in old age developing an upright-oval to rounded outline; dark, glossy green summer foliage, changing to superior shades of yellow, orange, scarlet and purple in fall; dark gray, at times almost black, bark which develops a block-like or "alligator hide" appearance (722); bluish oblong fruits which are ravaged by the birds (723); prefers acid, moist, deep soils; difficult to transplant; superior specimen tree; 30 to 50' by 20 to 30', can grow 80 to 100'; Zone 4.

Ostrya virginiana — American Hophornbeam

725

724

727

726

728

Pyramidal in youth (724), developing into a very graceful small tree with many horizontal or drooping branches, usually forming a rounded outline (725); medium green summer foliage, turning a
poor yellow in fall; winter habit is often exquisite (726, 727); bark is grayish brown, often broken
with narrow, longitudinal strips which are free at the end (728); pest-free tree; good specimen for
lawns, park, streets, golf courses; 25 to 40', two-thirds of, or equal to, that in spread; Zone 4.

Oxydendrum arboreum — Sourwood, Sorrel Tree, Lily-of-the-valley Tree

730

729

In youth often somewhat loose and open, developing into a pyramidal specimen with rounded top and drooping branches (729); lustrous, dark green summer foliage, often brilliant scarlet in fall, white fragrant flowers literally cover the canopy in June-July (730); requires well-drained, acid, organic soils; superior specimen plant where it can be grown; 20 to 30' by 20', can grow 50 to 75'; Zone 5, possibly 4.

Pachysandra procumbens — Alleghany Pachysandra

731

Low-growing, deciduous to semi-evergreen ground cover (731); dark, bluish green foliage; valuable and interesting substitute for *Pachysandra terminalis*; similar to *P. terminalis* in cultural requirements; 10 to 12" high; Zone 4.

Pachysandra terminalis — Japanese Pachysandra

Evergreen ground cover (732, 733); new foliage is a lovely light green, eventually changing to lustrous dark green; prefers loose, well-drained, acid soil; very shade-tolerant ground cover, unexcelled if given proper cultural conditions; 6 to 12'' high; Zone 4.

Parrotia persica — Persian Parrotia

734

735

736

737

738

Small, low-branched tree (734) or large multistemmed shrub (735) with an oval-rounded head of upright ascending branches; emerging leaves are reddish purple, changing to lustrous green (736) in summer; fall color often brilliant shades of yellow, orange and scarlet; older branches develop mottled patterns of gray, green, white and brown (737, 738): extremely pest-resistant; very adaptable; a most exquisite, small specimen plant; 20 to 40' by 15 to 30'; Zone 4.

Parthenocissus quinquefolia — Virginia Creeper or Woodbine

739

Deciduous vine with 5 to 8 branched tendrils, each tendril ending in adhesive-like tips; has the ability to literally cement itself to any structure (739) and requires no support; deep green summer foliage, changing to yellow, purple and red in fall; bluish black fruits in September-October; excellent, tough, low-maintenance vine for walls, trellises, rock piles; one of the first plants to show fall coloration; 30 to 50′ and more; Zone 3.

Parthenocissus tricuspidata — Japanese Creeper or Boston Ivy

740

741

Similar to above in all respects (740), except the leaves are simple and three-lobed (741); possibly not as hardy (Zone 4) but otherwise similar.

Paulownia tomentosa — Royal Paulownia

742

743

Rounded crown of rather coarse branches and large leaves (742); dark green summer foliage; interesting, pale violet, trumpet-shaped, fragrant flowers (743) in April before the leaves; adaptable and has almost become a weed in the south; too coarse for the average landscape but has possibilities for parks, golf courses and other large areas; 30 to 40' (and larger); Zone 5.

Paxistima canbyi — Canby Paxistima
(formerly spelled *Pachistima*)

744

Low-growing evergreen shrub with decumbent branches which often root when in contact with soil; relatively neat and compact (744); lustrous, dark green foliage, becoming bronzish in winter; prefers well-drained soil; somewhat susceptible to scale; good groundcover, facer plant; once established requires little attention; 1 to 2' by 3 to 5'; Zone 5.

Phellodendron amurense — Amur Corktree

745

747

748

746

Broad-spreading tree with a short trunk and an open rounded crown of a few large, ascending to horizontally arranged branches (745, 746); one of the most interesting trees for habit; shiny, deep green summer foliage, changing to yellow or bronzy yellow in fall and briefly persisting; interesting corky bark patterns (747, 748); black fruits on female trees; very adaptable species, withstanding acid and alkaline soils, drought and polluted air; valuable specimen because of unique, almost oriental, growth habit; 30 to 45' with an equal or greater spread; Zone 3.

Philadelphus coronarius — Sweet Mockorange

749

750

751

Large, often rounded shrub with stiff, straight, ascending branches; arching with age and often leggy, straggly (749); summer foliage is a flat green; flowers are the only ornamental aspect (750, 751), being white, fragrant and usually plentiful in late May through early June; old favorite for sweetly scented flowers but does not have much to recommend it for the modern landscape; 10 to 12' by 10 to 12'; Zone 4.

Photinia villosa — Oriental Photinia

752

754

753

Large shrub (752), developing a vase-shaped outline; can be grown as a small tree; dark green summer foliage; wine-red fall color; white flowers in May (753); red fruit in August-September; unfortunately very susceptible to fireblight (754); nice in groupings but the fireblight problem limits its use; 10 to 15'; Zone 4.

Physocarpus opulifolius — Common or Eastern Ninebark

755

756

757

Upright spreading shrub with stiffly recurved branches; rounded and dense in foliage (755) but ragged in winter; flat green summer foliage, poor yellowish to bronzish fall color; bark exfoliating into papery shreds (756); white or pinkish flowers in May (757); fruit a reddish capsule; extremely durable plant but lacking in ornamental attributes; quite coarse and difficult to use in the small home landscape; 5 to 9' by 6 to 10'; Zone 2.

Picea abies — Norway Spruce

759

758

760

761

762

764

763

Stiffly pyramidal in youth, with time developing pendulous branchlets and an overall soft, pyramidal outline (758); lustrous, dark green needles; spruces as a group prefer moderately moist, well-drained soil, although perform admirably under hot dry conditions of midwest; will make a fine specimen or windbreak; often overplanted; seed-grown plants show considerable variation; numerous cultivars have arisen, including 'Inversa' (759, 760), a weeping type; 'Nidiformis' has a bird's nest shape when young (761), changing drastically with time (762); 'Pendula', a weeping, sprawling, crawling sort, can be trained to individual specifications (763); 'Viminalis' has long pendulous branchlets (764); 50 to 60' by two-thirds that in spread, can grow to 100'; Zone 2.

Picea glauca — White Spruce

765

766

767

768

Dense pyramid in youth, becoming a tall, fairly dense, narrow spire with compact, regular, horizontal and ascending branches (765); glaucous green evergreen needles; other spruces are more handsome, however, this will withstand cold and hot dry conditions; makes a respectable hedge (766); 'Conica' is a densely pyramidal (767), slow-growing form (2 to 4″ per year) with short, radiating, light glaucous green needles; occasionally it will revert back to the type (768); 75 to 90′ by 12 to 15′, however, seldom reaches these heights in the midwest; Zone 2.

Picea mariana 'Doumetii' — Doumet Black Spruce

769

A superior selection compared to the species (769); maintains dense, broad, pyramidal shape; interesting bluish green foliage; could be effectively used as a specimen or accent plant; the species is often open, straggly and irregular; 10 to 15′ by 10 to 15′; Zone 2.

Picea omorika — Serbian Spruce

770

771

772

A beautiful evergreen tree with a remarkably slender trunk and short, ascending or drooping branches, forming a very narrow, pyramidal head (770); lustrous, dark green needles with whitish bands on the under side; needles are flat rather than angled, like those of most spruces; makes a beautiful specimen plant on smaller properties, handsome in groupings; 'Nana' (771) is a dwarf, densely conical bush of compact habit; 'Pendula' (772) is a beautiful spreading form which can be used as a ground cover; 50 to 60' by 20 to 25' (after 50 to 60 years); Zone 4.

Picea orientalis — Oriental Spruce

773

774

Extremely handsome, densely pyramidal evergreen in youth (773), developing slightly pendulous branches with age (774) and assuming a stately refined character; lustrous, dark green needles; as a specimen tree, much superior to *Picea abies* and *P. glauca*; highly recommended; 50 to 60' (after 70 to 80 years); Zone 5.

Picea pungens var. *glauca* — Blue Colorado Spruce

775

776

777

A broad, dense, regular pyramid (775) with horizontal stiff branches to the ground; becoming open, poor and dingy with age; needles range from blue-green to silver-blue (776) in color; performs well under very dry conditions; popular specimen plant but overused; tends to detract from other parts of the landscape; 'Pendula' (777) is a weeping form which, if not trained, develops into a sprawly mass of blue; 30 to 60' by 10 to 20' (can grow 90 to 130'); Zone 2.

Pieris floribunda — Mountain Pieris

778

Handsome, broadleaf evergreen shrub of neat bushy habit (778), low-rounded with rather stiff branches and dense foliage to the ground; dark green foliage; white flowers in April; very handsome native shrub which is limitedly available in commerce; 2 to 6' by 2 to 6' (or greater); Zone 4.

Pieris japonica — Japanese Pieris

779

780

781

782

Upright, broadleaf evergreen shrub of neat habit (779) with stiff spreading branches and dense, rosette-like foliage (780); sometimes developing a rounded-mounded outline (781); new growth a rich bronze, changing to lustrous dark green at maturity; urn-shaped, weakly fragrant flowers (782) occur in late March through early April and remain effective for two to three weeks; prefers acid, moist, well-drained soil and protection from desiccating winter wind; excellent foundation or shrub border plant; lacewing fly can be a serious problem; 9 to 12' by 6 to 8'; Zone 5(4).

Pinus aristata — Bristlecone Pine

783 784

Dwarf, shrubby, picturesque evergreen (783); dark green to bluish green needles which are covered by resinous exudations (784); does not perform well in the midwest; suitable for rock garden or accent plant; very slow-growing and could be used in the foundation planting; to 15' but only after many years; Zone 4.

Pinus banksiana — Jack Pine

785

Pyramidal in youth; open, spreading, often irregularly spreading and flat-topped in old age (785); dark green needles in summer, in winter often becoming yellow-green; not especially ornamental but valuable for windbreaks, shelterbelts and mass plantings in poor soils; valued for its cold hardiness; 35 to 50' (known to 70'), irregularly spreading but usually less than the height; Zone 2.

Pinus bungeana — Lacebark Pine

786

787

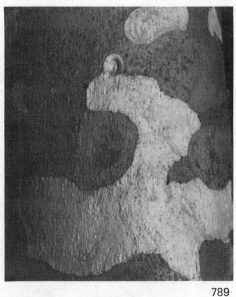

788

789

Pyramidal to pyramidal-oval or rounded (786), often with many trunks in youth (787); becoming open, picturesque with age; lustrous, bright green needles; bark exfoliates in patches like a plane tree (788), young branches greenish with irregular whitish or brownish areas interspersed (789); a quality specimen plant, servicable in most landscapes; 30 to 50' by 20 to 35'; Zone 4.

Pinus cembra — Swiss Stone Pine

A narrow, densely columnar pyramid in youth (790), opening with age (791); lustrous, dark, bluish green needles; very beautiful pine of slow growth; best suited for specimen use; 30 to 40', occasionally 70', with a 15 to 25' spread; Zone 2.

Pinus densiflora — Japanese Red Pine

794

796

797

795

798

Weakly pyramidal in youth (792), often shrubby; with age the trunks are frequently picturesquely crooked or leaning, branches horizontally spreading, resulting in a broad flat crown (793); bright green needles; orangish brown, scaly bark (794); makes a handsome, artistic, unusual specimen evergreen; 'Oculis-draconis' (795) has each needle marked with alternating green and yellow areas; 'Pendula' (796) is a weeping form; 'Unbraculifera' (797) is a mushroom to umbrella-shaped, cloud-like, multistemmed variant with interesting branching (798) and orangish brown, scaly bark; 40 to 60' with similar spread; Zone 4.

Pinus flexilis — Limber Pine

799

800

801

Variable in habit, dense, broad (799) or upright pyramid in form (800); with maturity becoming low, broad and flat-topped; handsome, bluish green needles; quality specimen tree but very slow-growing; 'Glauca Pendula' (801) is a blue-foliaged, semi-weeping type; 30 to 50' by 15 to 35'; Zone 2.

Pinus mugo — Swiss Mountain Pine

802

803

804

Highly variable, ranging from almost tree-like (802) to broad-spreading and bushy (803) to prostrate (804); apparently widely variable over its native range and, depending on the seed source, one may end up with a tree or a dwarf shrub; lustrous, dark green needles; makes a splendid foundation plant, grouping or mass, providing one has the dwarf type; species may grow 15 to 20' (up to 75'), while the dwarf types, like var. *mugo* and var. *pumilio*, usually are less than 5 to 8'; Zone 2.

Pinus nigra subsp. *nigra* — Austrian Pine

806

805

808

809

807

Broad dense pyramid in youth (805), becoming a large, broad, flat-topped tree with a rough short trunk and low, stout, spreading branches (806); dark, lustrous green needles; handsome bark which develops gray or gray-brown, mottled, flattened ridges (807); very hardy species, withstands city conditions better than other pines; somewhat salt-tolerant; good specimen plant; 'Hornibrookiana' (808) is a very compact, dwarf and rounded form which maintains that character into old age (809); 50 to 60' by 20 to 40' (and more), can grow to 100'; Zone 4.

Pinus parviflora — Japanese White Pine

810

811

Dense conical pyramid when young, developing wide-spreading branches, a flat-topped head and picturesque character with age (810); distinct, bluish green needles; handsome, rich brown cones (811), persisting 6 to 7 years; choice, extremely graceful small conifer whose low stature and fine-textured foliage make it a perfect tree for the small place; shows good salt-tolerance; 25 to 50' with a similar spread at maturity; Zone 5.

Pinus ponderosa — Ponderosa or Western Yellow Pine

812

Narrow to broad-pyramidal to columnar when young (812); some trees forming an open narrow crown at maturity; dark, yellowish green needles; valuable forest tree but not recommended for areas outside of which it is native; useful for mass plantings and shelter belts; 60 to 100' by 25 to 30' under cultivation, 150 to 230' in the wild; Zone 5 (4).

Pinus resinosa — Red Pine

813

814

In youth a broad pyramid with branches to the ground (813); at maturity massive, broad-spreading, flat-topped with horizontal branches; lustrous, medium to dark green needles; develops scaly, reddish brown bark (814); prefers acid, sandy, loose soils to the heavy clays of the midwest; makes a respectable specimen but does not compare favorably to *Pinus nigra* subsp. *nigra* in the midwest; 60 to 100' by 20 to 40' (and greater); Zone 2.

Pinus rigida — Pitch Pine

815

816

817

Open irregular pyramid in youth, becoming gnarled and more irregular with age; photograph 815 shows an unusually fine speciment of Pitch Pine; dark, yellowish green needles; blocky, mottled, gray-brown bark (816); not highly ornamental but recommended for poor, dry, sandy soils, along roadsides and the seacoast; 'Little Giant' is a most unusual artificial cultivar with feathery spheres of needles (817); 50 to 80' by 30 to 50'; Zone 4.

Pinus strobus — Eastern White Pine

818

819

820

821

822

822A

823

824

In youth a symmetrical pyramid (818); opening with age into a large, picturesque, irregular, horizontally branching tree (819); overall a very fine-textured tree; usually bluish green needles but greatly variable; interesting branching pattern (820) and adaptability to pruning (821) make it a choice landscape plant; best growth is achieved on moist, fertile, acid, well-drained soils; 'Fastigiata' is narrowly upright and columnar when young (822), developing a wider character with age (822a) as the branches ascend at a 45° angle from the trunk; 'Globosa' (823) is a very interesting, broad-rounded clone, 'Pendula' (824) is a weeping type with long branches which sweep the ground, however, it must be trained to develop a leader; 50 to 80' by 20 to 40', can grow to 150'; Zone 3.

Pinus sylvestris — Scotch Pine

825

826

827

828

829

830

In youth an irregular pyramid (825) with short spreading branches, the lower soon dying; becoming with age very picturesque, open, wide-spreading and flat or round-topped, almost umbrella-shaped (826); bluish green needle color; orangish scaly bark (827); makes a good specimen because of unusual habit and interesting bark color; 'Fastigiata' (828) is a columnar form which often breaks up in ice and snow storms; 'Watereri' (829) is a slow-growing (10 to 15'), densely pyramidal to flat-topped form with bluish needles, developing a multistemmed habit (830) and handsome orangish bark; 30 to 60' by 30 to 40', can grow 80 to 90'; Zone 2.

Pinus thunbergii — Japanese Black Pine

831

832

Broadly pyramidal, irregular shape in youth (831) and old age, unless properly pruned (832); dark green needles; severely injured at −15° to −25°F; because of tolerance to salt spray, it is invaluable for seashore plantings and useful in stabilizing sand dunes; under landscape conditions 20 to 40' (to 80') with a variable spread; Zone 5.

Pinus virginiana — Virginia or Scrub Pine

834

833

Broad open pyramid, becoming flat-topped, the branches arising irregularly from the stem (833); yellow-green to dark green needles; easily distinguished from *P. banksiana* by spines on back of cone scales (834); good plant for stabilizing poor soils, especially those of clay composition; 15 to 40′ by 10 to 30′; Zone 4.

Pinus wallichiana — Himalayan Pine

835

836

837

Loosely and broadly pyramidal when young; graceful, wide-spreading and dense at maturity (835); grayish to bluish green, long, pendulous needles (836); handsome bark (837), somewhat similar to that of Austrian Pine; excellent specimen evergreen for large areas, very graceful in effect; 50 to 80'; Zone 5 (4), shows variable hardiness and selection for hardy forms in recommended.

Platanus x *acerifolia* — London Planetree
(formerly *P.* x *hybrida*)

838

839

840

Pyramidal in youth, developing a large, open, wide-spreading outline with massive branches in age; extensively utilized in large-scale plantings (838); winter character is impressive (839), especially the olive-green, exfoliating bark (840); this tree has been overplanted; does not have superior summer or fall foliage but is tolerant of adverse cultural conditions and resistant to anthracnose, which afflicts *P. occidentalis*; 70 to 100' by 65 to 80'; Zone 4.

Platanus occidentalis — American Planetree, also know as Sycamore, Buttonwood and Buttonball-tree

841

842

843

844

Tree with a large trunk and a wide-spreading, open crown of massive crooked branches (841); a striking and impressive specimen, especially in winter when the white mottled bark stands out against the cold winter sky (842, 843); bark often develops interesting mottled character (844); summer foliage on all species is a flat, medium green, while fall color is yellow-tan-brown and unrewarding; quite susceptible to anthracnose, which blights the leaves and kills young stems; requires moist deep soils and here attains its greatest size; not recommended for the small or urban landscape; 70 to 100' by 70 to 100' (known to 150'); Zone 4.

Platanus orientalis — Oriental Planetree

846

845

847

Similar to *P.* x *acerifolia* in many respects (845), except the leaves (846) are more deeply incised and the fruits are borne 3 to 6 at a time, rarely in 2's (847): one of the parents of *P.* x *acerifolia* and carries anthracnose resistance; interesting tree but not sufficiently hardy in northern areas; Zone 7 (6).

Polygonum aubertii — Silvervine Fleeceflower

848

Twining deciduous vine (848) of rampant growth, often as much as 10 to 15' in one season; bright green summer foliage; white to slightly pinkish flowers in July-September; extremely adaptable and good for poor-soil areas; good on unsightly structures, fences, rock piles; 25 to 35'; Zone 4.

Polygonum cuspidatum compactum — Compact Japanese Fleeceflower (or *P. reynoutria*)

849

850

851

Low-growing, almost herbaceous plant (849) which spreads rapidly and quickly overtakes an area; new leaves (850) are reddish tinged, developing to medium green at maturity; flowers are greenish white and unattractive, but the reddish fruits are readily apparent in September-October (851); makes a good filler but is almost weedlike and can take over the garden in short order; 2' high and spreads indefinitely; Zone 4.

Poncirus trifoliata — Hardy or Trifoliate Orange

852

853

854

Small oval shrub or tree (852) with green spiny stems (853); foliage is dark green, changing to yellow in fall; flowers (854) are white, fragrant, borne on leafless stems in late April—early May; fruit is a large yellow berry; limitedly hardy in the north but an interesting novelty; good hedge or barrier; 15 to 20'; Zone 5.

Populus alba — Silver or White Poplar

855

856

Usually a wide-spreading tree with an irregular, broad, round-topped crown (855); spreading abundantly by root suckers; tends to be weak-wooded and susceptible to storm damage; foliage is a lustrous, dark green above, silvery white beneath; bark on young trees is a light, greenish gray or whitish, developing blackish areas with age; almost a weed but does quite well in wet areas; 'Pyramidalis' is a valuable columnar form (856) which can prove quite functional in the landscape; 40 to 70' high, variable spread; Zone 3.

Populus deltoides — Cottonwood, also called Eastern Poplar

857

858

859

Pyramidal in youth, developing a broad, vase-shaped habit in old age (857, 858) with the branching structure being somewhat open, irregular and ragged; summer foliage a lustrous green; quite dirty as it is always dropping twigs and leaves; bark (859) is ash-gray and divided into thick, flattened or rounded ridges, separated by deep fissures on old trunks; not a landscape tree unless nothing else will grow; found along water courses throughout the midwest and plains states; 75 to 100' by 50 to 75'; Zone 2.

Populus grandidentata — Bigtooth Aspen

860

861

Often pyramidal in youth with a central leader (860), developing an oval, open irregular crown at maturity; flat, medium green summer foliage; large serrations (861) give rise to the common name; very fast-growing (65' in 20 years); not a landscape tree but valuable for quick cover and pulp wood; 50 to 70' by 20 to 40'; Zone 3.

Populus nigra 'Italica' — Lombardy Poplar

862

863

Distinctly columnar, fast-growing, weedy cultivar (862) of limited value in modern landscapes; still widely sold and often seen gracing farmsteads; susceptible to an incurable canker disease which often initiates in upper and middle branches (863); 70 to 90' by 10 to 15' in 20 to 30 years but seldom lives this long; Zone 4.

Populus tremuloides — Quaking Aspen

864

Pyramidal and narrow when young, usually with a long trunk and narrow rounded crown at maturity (864); most widely distributed tree of North America; dark green summer foliage, often spectacular yellow in fall, which lights up the mountains of the west; leaves flutter in the slightest breeze, hence the common name; greenish gray bark; indifferent as to soil conditions; ornamentally not important because of disease and insect problems; used for pulp wood; 40 to 50' by 20 to 30'; Zone 1.

Populus tremula 'Erecta' — Erect European Aspen

865

Possible substitute for Lombardy Poplar; distinctly columnar (865); difficult to propagate and in central Illinois contracts leaf spot, which results in premature defoliation in August; possibly valuable in the more northernly climates; 30 to 50' by 8 to 15'; Zone 2.

Potentilla fruticosa — Bush Cinquefoil

866 867

868

869

Very bushy shrub with upright slender stems forming a low, rounded to broad-rounded outline (866, 867); summer foliage varies from gray to bright green; flowers are a bright, buttercup-yellow (actually vary from white to deep yellow and red), initiate in June and continue until frost; flowers on new wood and, unless rejuvenated every 2 or 3 years, becomes straggly and ineffective; excellent plant for summer color; valuable in mass (868, 869), groups, borders; trouble-free, hardy, tolerant; 1 to 4' by 2 to 4'; Zone 2.

Prinsepia sinensis — Cherry Prinsepia

871

870

Haystack to rounded, dense, spiny shrub (870), well-adapted for hedges (871) and screens; bright green summer color; one of the earliest shrubs to leaf out in the spring; flowers light yellow on previous year's wood in March-April; fruit a cherry-like drupe, ripening in July-August; easily cultured; valuable for hedges, screens, barriers, large areas; 6 to 10' by 6 to 10'; Zone 4.

Prinsepia uniflora — Hedge Prinsepia

872

Rather thorny, moderately dense aggregate of light gray branches (872); dark green summer foliage; yellow flowers; purplish red fruits; worthwhile hedge or barrier; seldom seen in gardens; 4 to 5' by 4 to 5'; Zone 4.

Prunus avium — Mazzard Cherry

873

874

875

Large tree of conical shape (873) which produces liberal quantities of fragrant white flowers (874) in April; the emerging leaves are tinged bronze-purple, deep green in summer, changing to yellow and bronze in fall; from this species the popular sweet cherries have been developed; bark (875) shows typical cherry characteristics; *Prunus*, as a group, suffers from numerous insects and diseases; a well-drained soil of average nature is acceptable; *Prunus* are usually planted for their beautiful flowers; 'Plena' has double, white, 1 to 1½'' diameter flowers and is superior to the species; 30 to 40' by 30 to 40'; Zone 3.

Prunus cerasifera 'Atropurpurea' — Purpleleaf Plum

877

876

878

Small shrubby tree (876), often twiggy and rounded with ascending spreading branches (877); foliage is reddish purple and, depending on the cultivar, may stay vivid throughout the summer; flowers are pinkish, fragrant and occur in April before the leaves (878); principal landscape attraction is the purple foliage; often overused; susceptible to insects and diseases; short-lived; 15 to 25' by 15 to 25'; Zone 3.

Prunus glandulosa — Dwarf Flowering Almond

879

881

880

Bargain basement shrub of many discount stores; develops into a weakly spreading, multistemmed, straggly shrub (879); light green summer foliage; double, 1 to 1½″ diameter, pinkish white flowers offer landscape interest in late April to early May (880, 881); plant has limited appeal for modern landscapes; 4 to 5′ by 4 to 5′; Zone 4.

Prunus 'Hally Jolivette'

882

Rounded, densely branching, small, shrubby tree (882) of relatively fine texture; result of a cross between *P. subhirtella* x *P. yedoensis*, crossed back on *P. subhirtella*; flowers are pink in bud, opening white, double, 1 to 1¼'' diameter and effective over a 10 to 20-day period in late April to early May; very worthwhile plant for the shrub border; 15'; Zone 5.

Prunus laurocerasus — Laurel Cherry

883

The species is a large, wide-spreading, broadleaf evergreen shrub (883); foliage is a lustrous black-green; flowers are white; fruits purple to black; 'Otto Luyken' is a dwarf form which grows 3 to 5' by 6 to 8'; in general not adaptable to northern areas but is quite popular in the south; may grow 10 to 18' high; Zone 6, preferably 7.

Prunus maackii — Amur Chokecherry

884

885

886

887

Pyramidal to rounded, often multistemmed (884), densely branched tree (885); good, dark green summer foliage; white flowers occur in 2 to 3'' long racemes in early to mid-May; the bark is a rich brownish yellow (886) and peels off in strips (887), similar to that of some birches; worthwhile for winter bark color; 30 to 45'; Zone 2.

Prunus padus — European Birdcherry

888

889

Low-branched, often multistemmed small tree or large shrub of rounded outline (888); dull, dark green summer foliage, followed by yellow to bronze leaves in the fall; fragrant white flowers are borne in liberal quantities from mid-April to early May (889); this is the first tree to leaf-out on the University of Illinois campus and the new leaves are a welcome sight after a difficult midwestern winter; performs well in the midwest; perhaps should be considered for more extensive use; makes a handsome specimen or grouping; 30 to 40' by 30 to 40'; Zone 3.

Prunus persica — Common Peach

890

891

892

893

Habit is best described as one of ascending limbs, forming a low, broad, globular crown (890, 891); flowers are principal assets and range from single (892) to double (893) in a variety of colors from white to deepest red; very susceptible to diseases and insects; short-lived in most landscape situations; 15 to 25'; Zone 5.

Prunus sargentii — Sargent Cherry

894

895

Tree with ascending branches (894), developing a rounded crown at maturity; new leaves are reddish, changing to lustrous dark green in summer and finally bronze or red in fall; lustrous reddish or mahogany brown bark; flowers are single, pink, 1 to 1½" across and occur in late April to early May; fruit is a purple-black drupe; excellent specimen cherry which seems quite tolerant of adverse conditions; 'Columnaris' is a narrow upright form (895); perhaps the best of the large cherries for ornamental use; 40 to 50'; Zone 4.

Prunus serotina — Black Cherry

897

896

898

Often considered a weed tree; in youth loosely pyramidal (896), in old age developing an oval crown of pendulous branches; shiny, dark green summer foliage, yellow to reddish in fall; bark is scaly, grayish brown or black (897); white racemose flowers in May; interesting red to black fruits (898) in August to September, can be used for wines and jellies; wood is valuable for furniture production; not a tree worth adding to the landscape but, if present, certainly do not remove; 50 to 60'; Zone 3.

Prunus serrula

899

A small vigorous tree growing to 30'; main asset is the glistening surface of the polished, reddish brown, mahogany-like bark (899); difficult to find commercially but worth seeking; Zone 5.

Prunus serrulata 'Kwanzan' — Kwanzan Oriental Cherry

900

901

902

There are many cultivars of this species, but 'Kwanzan' has proven popular in the midwest; basically a vase-shaped habit (900) with a rounded or flat-topped crown (901); new foliage is reddish-tinged, eventually changing to lustrous, dark green in summer and finally yellow to bronze in fall; flowers are double (902), pink, late April to early May and freely borne; not a long-lived tree but certainly beautiful in flower; usually grafted on *P. avium* at height of 4 to 6'; 20 to 25'; Zone 5, 'Kwanzan' is perhaps the most cold-hardy.

Prunus subhirtella — Higan Cherry

903

904

905

906

907

908

910

909

The exact nature of the species is difficult to discern but is basically rounded in outline (903); 'Autumnalis' is a semi-double form, sporadically flowering in fall, remaining flowers opening in spring (904); 'Pendula' (905, 906) is a popular form with pink flowers before the leaves in April, foliage a handsome, lustrous green in summer, habit offering good summer (907) and winter (908) landscape interest; 'Yae-shidare-higan' (909, 910) is a double-flowered, pink form; 20 to 40' with a spread of 15 to 30' or more; Zone 5.

Prunus tomentosa — Manchu or Nanking Cherry

911

912

913

Broad-spreading, densely twiggy shrub (911), becoming more open and irregular with age; medium green summer foliage (912); reddish brown bark develops an exfoliating characteristic; fragrant, pinkish in bud, finally white (913) flowers in early to mid-April; fruits are scarlet, ½'' across, edible and ripen in June-July; valuable for early flowers and fruit but otherwise too coarse for the modern landscape; 6 to 10' by 15'; Zone 2.

Prunus triloba — Flowering Plum, Flowering Almond

914

915

Large, cumbersome, clumsy, ragged shrub (914) which appears rather ill-kempt except when in flower; medium green summer foliage, turning yellow to bronze in fall; flowers are double, pink, 1 to 1½'' across and occur before the leaves in late April (915); probably best used in mass, as single specimens appear out-of-place; 12 to 15' by 12 to 15'; Zone 5.

Prunus virginiana — Common Chokecherry

916

918

917

Small tree or large shrub with crooked branches and slender twigs, forming an oval-rounded crown (916); has a tendency to sucker and can develop large thickets; foliage is a flat, dark green; flowers are white (917) and rather attractive in late April; fruits are dark purple; easily grown but not recommended for the average landscape; 'Shubert' (918) is a pyramidal-rounded form with dense foliage, green at first, finally reddish purple; 20 to 30' by 18 to 35'; Zone 2.

Prunus yedoensis — Yoshino Cherry

919

921

920

Handsome, broad-rounded, horizontally branched tree (919); good, dark green summer foliage; single, white to pink, slightly fragrant flowers in April-May (920); bark is interesting (921); worthwhile tree but probably best where winters are not extremely harsh; 20 to 30' by 25 to 40'; Zone 5, preferably 6.

Pseudolarix kaempferi — Golden-larch
(formerly *P. amabilis*)

922

923

924

Broad-pyramidal, deciduous conifer with wide-spreading, horizontal branches (922) and a rather open outline at maturity; bright green summer foliage, borne in clusters of 15 to 30 needles which change to golden yellow in fall (923), abscising soon thereafter; mature, golden to reddish brown cones are beautiful; bark platy, grayish brown (924); requires acid, moist, well-drained soil; beautiful specimen tree of unusual character; 30 to 50′ by 20 to 40′; Zone 5.

Pseudotsuga menziesii — Douglasfir

925

926

927

An open, spire-like pyramid with straight stiff branches, the lower drooping, upper ascending; dense in youth (925), becoming loose, open and ragged with age (926); bluish green needles on the hardy types; prefers areas where moisture is abundant; does acceptably in midwest and east, growing 30 or 40'; principal landscape value is as a specimen; 'Fastigiata' (927) is a dense, good-looking, conical form; 40 to 80' by 12 to 20'; Zone 5 (4).

Ptelea trifoliata — Hoptree, Wafer-ash, Stinking-ash

928

929

Small tree or, more often, a large multistemmed shrub (928); lustrous, dark green summer foliage; fruits are compressed, broad-winged samaras (929); very adaptable species; of value only in a native situation; 15 to 20'; Zone 4.

Pterocarya fraxinifolia — Caucasian Wingnut

930

932

931

Broad-spreading, rounded tree, often branched close to the ground (930); handsome, lustrous, dark green summer foliage (931); fruits (932) are winged nutlets; little-known tree, worthy of increased use; 30 to 50' with a similar or greater spread; Zone 5.

Pterostyrax hispidus — Fragrant Epaulette Tree

933

A round-headed, small tree which develops an open crown (933) with slender spreading branches; bright green summer foliage; white fragrant flowers on 5 to 10" long, pendulous panicles in June; requires moist, well-drained, acid soil; difficult to locate in commerce but worth considering for the small residential landscape; 20 to 30' with a similar spread; Zone 6.

Pyracantha coccinea — Firethorn

934

935

937

936

Semi-evergreen to evergreen shrub with stiff thorny branches and an open habit if left unpruned; usually maintained as a dense shrub (934); lustrous, dark green summer foliage, becoming brownish in extremely cold or exposed areas; white flowers in late May or early June; superior orange-red fruits (935) in September which persist into late fall; makes an excellent espalier plant (936) for it withstands heavy pruning; good bank cover (937), mass, wall covering; susceptible to fireblight and scab (fruits); best to prune to required dimensions; 6 to 18' in height; Zone 5 (6), select cultivars ('Lalandei', 'Chadwickii', 'Kasan', 'Wyattii') of proven hardiness for northern areas.

Pyrus calleryana — Callery Pear

938

939

940

941

942

943

944

945

946

The species (938) is a broad-pyramidal tree with glossy, dark green foliage but is considered inferior to the cultivars; 'Bradford' (939) has malodorous, showy, white flowers in late April-early May (940), excellent, lustrous, dark green summer foliage, brilliant reddish purple fall colors (941) and uniquely conical outline, makes an excellent street tree or screen (942, 943), is very adaptable and quite tolerant of city conditions, thus highly recommended; 'Aristocrat' is a rather open form (944) with more horizontal branch development, leaves having a wavy margin (945) and supposedly coloring a uniform reddish purple in the fall; 'Chancellor' (946) is a conical form with distinctly ascending branches; all cultivars are handsome plants and will probably grow 30 to 50' with a variable spread; Zone 4.

Pyrus communis — Common Pear

947

949

948

Pyramidal to oval (947) in outline; glossy green summer foliage, often purplish in fall; white malo-dorous flowers (948) in June; has been used for espaliers on walls (949); tremendous fireblight susceptibility and therefore not recommended; 30 to 50'; Zone 5.

Quercus acutissima — Sawtooth Oak

950

Dense broad pyramid in youth (950); varying in old age from oval-rounded to broad-rounded; dark, lustrous green summer foliage, potentially a good clear yellow in fall; susceptible to iron chlorosis; not widely used but valuable as a specimen or shade tree; 35 to 45'; Zone 6 (5).

Quercus alba — White Oak

951

952

953

954

Pyramidal in youth (951), upright-rounded (952) to broad-rounded with wide-spreading branches at maturity; very imposing specimen when fully grown; leaves are grayish to pinkish when unfolding, changing to dark, almost blue-green in summer (953); fall color varies from brown to rich wine-red or purple in fall; bark is ashy gray, often developing flat gray areas (954); makes a valuable specimen tree but is difficult to transplant; wood is valuable; 50 to 80' by 50 to 80' (can grow over 100'); Zone 4.

Quercus bicolor — Swamp White Oak

955

956

Pyramidal in youth (955), forming a broad, open, round-topped crown and short "limby" trunk with maturity (956); lustrous, dark green summer foliage, sometimes yellow-brown in fall; prefers moist soils and is quite susceptible to chlorosis; somewhat difficult to transplant; not a common landscape tree; 50 to 60' with an equal or greater spread; Zone 3.

Quercus coccinea — Scarlet Oak

957

958

Pyramidal in youth (957), somewhat similar to Pin Oak in outline but more rounded and open at maturity (958); excellent, glossy green summer foliage, often followed by intense scarlet fall coloration; difficult to transplant and seldom seen in midwestern landscapes; 70 to 75' by 40 to 50'; Zone 4.

Quercus imbricaria — Shingle Oak

959

960

Pyramidal to upright-oval in youth (959), assuming a broad-rounded outline in old age (960); dark green summer foliage, changing yellow-brown to russet-red in fall; transplants with less difficulty than many oaks; makes a nice specimen or shade tree where there is ample room for development; often holds leaves late into winter; 50 to 60' by 50 to 60' or greater; Zone 4.

Quercus macrocarpa — Bur Oak, Mossycup Oak

961

962

Weakly pyramidal to oval in youth, gradually developing a massive trunk (961) and a broad crown of stout branches (962); lustrous, dark green summer foliage; difficult to transplant and slow-growing; best reserved for natural areas; 70 to 80' by 70 to 80'; Zone 2.

Quercus muehlenbergii — Chinkapin Oak

963

Weakly rounded in youth but of dapper outline; with maturity developing an open rounded crown (963); dark, lustrous green summer foliage; fall color varies from yellow to orangish brown to brown; good tree for dry, limestone-based soils; seldom available in commerce; 40 to 50' by 40 to 50'; Zone 5.

Quercus palustris — Pin Oak, Swamp Oak

964

965

966

Strongly pyramidal, usually with a central leader; the lower branches pendulous, the middle horizontal and the upper ascending (924); becoming more pyramidal-oval with age (965); dark glossy green in summer, changing to russet, bronze or red in fall; very popular oak and quite easy to transplant; widely used as a lawn and street tree; extremely susceptible to iron chlorosis; 'Sovereign' (966) does not develop the weeping lower branches; 60 to 70' by 25 to 40'; Zone 4.

Quercus phellos — Willow Oak

967

968

A graceful, fine-textured, softly pyramidal tree (967) in youth; developing a dense, oblong to oval crown at maturity (968); rich green summer foliage, changing to yellow and russet-red in fall; prefers moist, acid soils; very handsome tree which is widely used in the south; best reserved for southern areas of the midwest; 40 to 60' by 30 to 40'; Zone 6.

Quercus robur — English Oak

969

970

972

971

Pyramidal to rounded in youth (969), developing a large, massive, broadly rounded, open-headed crown with a short trunk at maturity (970); dark green to bluish green summer foliage, holding into November; adaptable species which performs quite well in high-pH soils; best reserved for parks and other large areas; 'Fastigiata' (971) is a functional upright form which can be effectively integrated into small and large landscapes (972); 75 to 100' with a similar spread; Zone 4.

Quercus rubra — Red Oak

974

973

975

976

Rounded in youth and old age, often round-topped and symmetrical (973); young foliage a soft feathery reddish (974), changing to lustrous, dark green in summer and varying from brown to russet-red to rich red in fall; bark develops flat gray areas (975); male flowers of red oak (and all oaks) are borne in bead-like, pendulous catkins (976); valuable oak; widely used in landscapes for it transplants easily; used as street or lawn tree; 60 to 75' by 40 to 50'; Zone 4.

Rhamnus cathartica — Common Buckthorn

977

978

Large shrub or small tree with a rounded bushy crown of crooked stoutish stems (977); lustrous, dark green (978), pest-resistant summer foliage; prolific black fruits in August; very tough tree, tolerant of adverse cultural conditions; suitable for areas where little else will grow; 18 to 25' by 18 to 25'; Zone 2.

Rhamnus frangula 'Columnaris' — Tallhedge Glossy Buckthorn

979

980

981

982

The species (979) is not employed in modern landscapes, however 'Columnaris' (980) has proven useful; it is a narrow, densely branched, columnar form which has received wide favor for screens, hedges, privacy barriers; effective in winter because of density of branching if properly maintained (981); glossy green summer foliage; red to purplish black fruits from July through September; 'Asplenifolia' (982) is a cutleaf form of rounded habit and very fine texture; 10 to 18' by 3 to 5'; Zone 2.

Rhododendron carolinianum — Carolina Rhododendron

983

984

Small rounded evergreen shrub (983) of rather gentle proportions; not as coarse as the Catawba hybrids; dark green summer foliage, assuming a purplish tinge in winter; flowers (984) vary from pure white to pale rose, rose and lilac-rose in color, May; lovely plant for the border but requires attention to cultural details: acid, moist, well-drained, cool soils and protection from extreme winter sun and sweeping winds; 3 to 6' by 3 to 6'; Zone 5.

Rhododendron catawbiense — Catawba Hybrid Rhododendrons

985

986

Heavy evergreen shrub with large dense foliage to the ground (985); often leggy in unfavorable locations; usually taller than wide, although it does assume a rounded appearance on occasion; dark green foliage, often yellow-green under the extremes of midwestern winters; hybrids vary in flower color from white, pink, rose and lavendar to red and are borne in large, 5 to 6" diameter clusters in mid to late May; superlative plants if given proper culture; select cold-hardy clones; functional in shrub borders, edges of woodlands (986) and other protected places; 6 to 10', rarely 15 to 20'; Zone 4.

Rhododendron 'Exbury Hybrids'

987

988

989

Deciduous, upright, relatively bushy azaleas (987); medium green summer foliage and yellow, orange, red fall colors; flowers (988, 989) range from creams, yellows and near whites to pink, rose, orange and red and are borne in 2 to 3'' diameter clusters in mid to late May; extremely floriferous and add brilliant color to the spring landscape; 6 to 10'; Zone 5.

Rhododendron x *laetevirens* — Wilson Rhododendron

990

Low-growing, mounded (990), glossy-leaved evergreen with pink to purplish flowers; nice plant for rock garden or foundation planting; not a particularly floriferous species; 2 to 4' by 2 to 6'; Zone 4.

Rhododendron mucronulatum — Korean Rhododendron

991

992

Deciduous shrub of upright-oval to rounded outline with clean branching pattern (991); soft green summer foliage, followed by shades of yellow and bronzy crimson in fall; flowers bright rosy purple (992), occuring on leafless stems in March; first of all hardy rhododendrons and azaleas to flower in northeastern United States; very lovely in the shrub border; flowers early and may be injured by frost; 4 to 8' with a similar spread; Zone 4.

Rhododendron 'P.J.M. Hybrids'

993

Basically haystack-shaped to rounded in outline (993); dark green summer foliage is plum-purple through the winter; vivid, bright lavendar-pink flowers in mid to late April; other colors now available, including white; good choice for cold climates; 3 to 6' by 3 to 6'; Zone 4.

Rhododendron schlippenbachii — Royal Azalea

994

995

996

Upright-rounded, deciduous shrub, often somewhat open; dark green summer foliage, appearing as if in whorls (994), changing to yellow, orange, crimson in fall; flowers pale to rose-pink (995, 996), fragrant, early to mid-May; one of the most delicate and lovely azaleas for northern gardens; recommended for the shrub border; 6 to 8' and as wide at maturity; Zone 4.

Rhodotypos scandens — Black Jetbead

997

998

999

1000

Mounded, loosely branched shrub with ascending and somewhat arching branches, often of shabby appearance (997); bright green summer foliage (998), holding late into fall (November); white flowers in May-June (999); shining black fruit (1000) ripens in October and persists into the following summer; very tough plant which tolerates poor soils, crowding, polluted conditions; full sun or shade; good hedge, mass, filler where other plants will not grow; 3 to 6' by 4 to 9'; Zone 4.

Rhus aromatica — Fragrant Sumac

1001

1002

1003

Low, irregular, spreading or mounded shrub with lower branches turning up at tips; tends to sucker from the roots and produces a dense tangled mass of stems (1001); glossy, blue-green foliage in summer, varying from yellow to orange to reddish purple in fall; yellowish flowers on leafless stems in March-April; red, hairy drupes (1002) in August-September; excellent plant for poor soils and shade; 'Gro-low' (1003) is a low, wide-spreading form with excellent glossy foliage, 2 to 4' high; species varies from 2 to 6' (and larger) with a spread of 6 to 10'; Zone 3.

Rhus chinensis — Chinese Sumac

1004

1005

Loose, spreading, suckering shrub (1004) or flat-headed tree; interesting bright green summer foliage (1005); yellowish white flowers occur in August-September; fruits are orange-red, maturing in October; best used in large areas, shrub border; of principal value for late flower; becomes rather gaunt in old age; not preferable to *R. copallina*, *R. glabra* or *R. typhina*; 24'; Zone 5.

Rhus copallina — Flameleaf or Shining Sumac

1006

1007

Compact and dense in extreme youth, becoming more and more open, irregular and picturesque as it ages, with crooked, ascending and spreading branches (1006); broader at the top; foliage is a lustrous dark green (1007) in summer, changing to rich red, crimson and scarlet in fall; fruits are crimson and ripen in September-October; one of the best sumacs for dry rocky soils; superior fall color; 20 to 30' with a similar spread; Zone 4.

Rhus glabra — Smooth Sumac

1008

1009

Irregular, spreading, suckering shrub (1008), developing in all directions from the mother plant; medium green summer foliage, changing to excellent yellow-orange-purple-red combinations in fall; fruit is a scarlet hairy drupe, borne in 6 to 10" long panicles and persisting (1009); good plant for massing, highways, and dry, poor-soil areas; 9 to 15', often smaller; Zone 2.

Rhus typhina — Staghorn Sumac

1011

1010

1012

1013

1014

A large, loose, open, spreading shrub or a gaunt scraggly tree (1010) with a flattish crown and rather picturesque branches (1011), resembling those of a male deer; dull to bright green summer foliage, changing to orange and scarlet in fall; handsome crimson fruits which persist into winter; tolerates very dry, sterile soil; suckers profusely and tends to form wide-spreading colonies; 'Laciniata' (1012, 1013) is a cut-leaf form of fine texture and does not grow as tall as the species (1014); 15 to 25' (30 to 40'), spreading indefinitely; Zone 3.

Ribes alpinum — Alpine Currant

1015

1016

Densely twiggy, rounded shrub; erect in youth with stiffly upright stems and spreading branches; bright green summer foliage; one of the first shrubs to leaf-out in the spring; scarlet fruits on female plants are seldom seen, as male plants predominate in cultivation; very tolerant of shade and less-than-ideal growing conditons; makes a superlative hedge plant (1015) or mass; 'Compactum' (1016) is a compact form about one-half the size of the species; 3 to 6' (and larger); Zone 2.

Ribes odoratum — Clove Currant

1017

1018

Irregular shrub of ascending arching stems, usually surrounded by a mass of suckers (1017); bright (almost bluish) green summer foliage, yellow to reddish purple in fall; yellow, clove-scented flowers (1018) in April; good shrub for border, however, rather unkempt; 6 to 8', irregularly spreading; Zone 4.

Robinia fertilis

1019

1020

Small, suckering, low-growing shrub (1019) of irregular proportions; bluish green summer foliage; scentless rose or pale purple flowers (1020) are borne in 2 to 4″ pendulous racemes in May-June; good plant for stabilizing sandy banks and dry, sterile, impoverished soils; *Robinia hispida*, Bristly Locust, is similar but does not fruit as heavily; 6 to 10′ by 6 to 10′, although can form large colonies due to suckering habit; Zone 5.

Robinia pseudoacacia — Black Locust

1021

1022

1023

1024

Often an upright tree with a straight trunk and a narrow oblong crown (1021, 1022), becoming ragged with age; will develop thickets, as it freely seeds and develops shoots from the roots; effective, blue-green summer foliage; fragrant white flowers (1023) in late May or early June; good plant for poor-soil areas as it fixes atmospheric nitrogen; 'Umbraculifera' (1024) forms a dense, umbrella-like canopy; 30 to 50' (70 to 80') by 20 to 35'; Zone 3.

Rosa rugosa — Rugosa Rose or Saltspray Rose

1025

1026

Sturdy shrub with stout upright stems, filling the ground and forming a dense cover (1025); lustrous rugose, deep green summer foliage, yellowish red or orange in fall, fragrant flowers vary from white to rose-purple, 2½ to 3½" across, from June through August; fruit (1026) is a 1" diameter, brick-red hip; excellent plant for sandy soils and areas where salts present a cultural problem; highly recommended for roadside plantings in northern states where poor soils and deicing salts are prevalent; 4 to 6' by 4 to 6'; Zone 2.

Rosa wichuriana — Memorial Rose

1027

A procumbent shrub of semi-evergreen nature (1027) with long green canes trailing over the ground and rooting; lustrous, dark green foliage; pure white, single, 2″ diameter flowers in June and July; red fruit, maturing in September-October; good plant for ground cover use, especially on banks, cuts and fills; worthwhile because of ease of culture and freedom from pests; ground cover or, if supported, 8 to 16′ climber; Zone 5.

Salix alba — White Willow

1029

1028

1030

1031

1032

Large, low-branching tree with long branches and flexible stems, forming a broad, open, round-topped crown (1028); summer foliage is bright green above, silvery beneath, changing to yellow-green in fall; bark (1029) is yellowish brown to brown, somewhat corky, ridged and furrowed; the species is seldom used in modern landscapes, 'Ovalis' (1030) is an oval-headed form, 'Tristis' (1031) a handsome weeping form with yellow stems in winter; willows have a place near water (1032) and in areas that are too wet for the successful culture of other plants; they are subject to numerous insects and diseases and require considerable care; 75 to 100' by 50 to 100'; Zone 2.

Salix babylonica — Babylon Weeping Willow

1033

1034

1035

A very graceful, refined tree (1033) with a short stout trunk and a broad rounded crown of weeping branches which sweep the ground; dark green summer foliage; stems are greenish; quite a lovely tree but not as hardy as *S. a.* 'Tristis'; 'Annularis' (1034) has semi-weeping branches and leaves (1035) with ram-horn configuration; 30 to 40' by 30 to 40'; Zone 6.

Salix caprea — Goat Willow

1036

1037

1038

1039

Small tree or large shrub (1036, 1037), often of unkempt habit because of various disease and insect problems; summer foliage is dark green; principal landscape asset is the male catkin (1038) which arrives before the leaves in March through early April; nice plant for forcing inside during late winter; 'Pendula' (1039) is a ground cover type or, when grafted on the species, makes a small specimen tree; 15 to 25' with a 12 to 15' spread; Zone 4.

Salix matsudana 'Tortuosa' — Contorted Hankow Willow

1040

1041

Usually a low-branched tree of oval to rounded outline (1040), developing spreading, contorted and twisted branches (1041); a popular plant with floral designers and this is probably its best use; not especially long-lived in the landscape; the branches are not as contorted as those of *Corylus avellana* 'Contorta'; 30', possibly 40'; Zone 4.

Salix pentandra — Laurel Willow

1042

1043

A compact, oval, low-branched tree (1042); the leaves are a lustrous, polished, shimmering dark green in summer (1043); often infected with leaf spot so severely that by August there are few leaves on the tree; 40 to 60'; Zone 4.

Salix purpurea — Purpleosier Willow

1044

1045

1046

Rounded, dense, finely branched shrub if properly maintained; bluish green summer foliage; needs rejuvenation to be kept in good condition: an older planting before (1044) and after (1045) rejuvenation is shown; worthwhile considering for wet areas but must be properly maintained; makes a good hedge (1046) and withstands pruning about as well as privet; 8 to 10' by 8 to 10'; Zone 4.

Salix sachalinense 'Sekka' — Japanese Fantail Willow

1047

1048

A curious shrub of rounded to broad-rounded outline (1047) which develops branches with distinct flattened areas (1048); summer foliage a lustrous bright green; the stems are a purplish brown and can be effectively used in arrangements; not wholesalely recommended by this author; although sometimes listed as a small tree, the largest I have seen were 10 to 12' high and shrubby; Zone 4.

Sambucus canadensis — American Elder

1049

1050

1051

Stoloniferous, multistemmed shrub, often broad and rounded with branches spreading and arching (1049); bright green summer foliage; flowers are white and borne in 6 to 10'' diameter, flat-topped cymes (1050) in June; the purple-black fruits (1051) mature in August-September and are used for jellies and wines; requires moist soils; can almost become a weed as the birds deposit the seed everywhere; not recommended for the modern landscape but has potential near wet areas, for roadside plantings and naturalizing; 5 to 12', spread quite variable; Zone 3.

Sassafras albidum — Common Sassafras

1052

1053

1054

1055

Pyramidal, irregular tree or shrub in youth with many short, stout, contorted branches (1052) which spread abruptly to form a flat-topped, irregular (1053), round-oblong head at maturity; often sprouting from roots and forming thickets (1054); bright to medium green summer foliage, changing to brilliant yellows, oranges, scarlets and purples in fall; bark is a dark reddish brown and deeply ridged and furrowed (1055); yellow fragrant flowers before the leaves in April; dark blue fruits in September, borne on scarlet fruit stalks; prefers acid, loamy, well-drained soil; difficult to transplant; excellent plant for naturalizing and roadsides; 30 to 60' by 25 to 40'; Zone 4.

Schizophragma hydrangeoides — Japanese Hydrangeavine

1057

1056

True clinging vine (1056) which develops roots along the stems and throughly cements itself to a porous support; dark green summer foliage (1057); flowers are white; Zone 5.

Sciadopitys verticillata — Umbrella-pine or Japanese Umbrella-pine

1058

1059

1060

1061

Compact, broadly pyramidal tree in youth (1058) with a straight stem and horizontal branches spreading in whorls; stiff and twiggy, the young branchlets with the leaves crowded at the ends (1059); glossy, dark green needles; bark develops a rich, reddish brown color and slight shreddy consistency (1060); prefers a rich, moist, acid soil and protection from hot sun and sweeping wind; nice plant for rock garden, accent or border (1061); quite slow-growing; hard to locate in midwestern nurseries; 20 to 30' by 15 to 20'; Zone 5.

Shepherdia argentea — Silver Buffaloberry

1062

A thorny shrub (1062), sometimes nearly tree-like; silvery summer foliage; yellow flowers; red fruits; will do well in poor soils and where salts present a problem; 6 to 10' (18'); Zone 2.

Shepherdia canadensis — Russet Buffaloberry

1063

Small, loosely branched shrub of rounded outline (1063); gray-green summer foliage; yellowish flowers in April to May; yellowish red fruits which are effective in June-July; has about the same uses as *S. argentea*; 6 to 8'; Zone 2.

Sophora japonica — Japanese Pagodatree or Scholar-tree

1064

1065

1066

1067

1068

Dense when young (1064), spreading, with a broadly rounded crown at maturity (1065); lustrous, medium to dark green summer foliage; creamy white, mildly fragrant flowers in late July through August (1066); interesting, bright green fruits (1067), changing to yellow and finally yellow-brown; very handsome specimen tree which does well under city conditions; makes a good shade tree; 'Pendula' (1068) is a weeping form; 50 to 75' high with a comparable spread; Zone 4.

Sorbaria sorbifolia — Ural Falsespirea

1069

1070

Stoloniferous shrub (1069), forming large colonies if left unchecked; one of the first shrubs to leaf-out in spring; new foliage has a reddish tint, eventually changing to deep green; white flowers (1070) are borne in 4 to 10″ panicles in late June into July; quite tolerant of any soil, however, prefers those that are moist, well-drained; good plant for shrub border, massing, grouping, bank covers; flowers on current season's growth so can be effectively renewal-pruned in spring; 5 to 10′ by 5 to 10′; Zone 2.

Sorbus alnifolia — Korean Mountainash

1071

1072

1073

1074

Pyramidal to oblong-headed tree (1071), somewhat reminiscent of *Fagus sylvatica* in outline; hand-some, rich green summer foliage (1072), changing to orange-red in fall; bark of old trunks is beech-like; while young, branches display diamond-shaped lenticels (1073); flowers are white, followed by orange-red fruits in August-September (1074); mountainashes as a group prefer well-drained soils and cool summer temperatures; perhaps the most adaptable of mountainashes; not as susceptible to borers as other species; fine specimen tree; 40 to 50' by 20 to 30'; Zone 4.

Sorbus aria — Whitebeam Mountainash

1075

1076

Broad-pyramidal or ovoid in outline (1075); leaves leathery, lustrous, dark green (upper surface), white tomentose (lower surface)(1076); fall coloration may vary from pale green to golden brown to reddish; white flowers in May; ½"diameter, orange-red or scarlet fruits in September-October; interesting tree, reserved for northern gardens; 35 to 45' high; Zone 5.

Sorbus aucuparia — European Mountainash

1077

1078

1079

Erect and oval in youth (1077), forming an ovate or spherical, gracefully open head at maturity (1078); flat green summer foliage; fall color varies from green to yellowish to reddish; white flowers in May; outstanding, orange-red fruit in August-September which literally weighs down the branches (1079); suffers from borers, fireblight; often short-lived in hot dry climates; best reserved for cold areas where it functions as a fine specimen plant; 20 to 40' by two-thirds that in width; Zone 3.

Sorbus discolor — Snowberry Mountainash

1080

1081

Rounded to broad-rounded tree (1080) with exceedingly large clusters of red fruit (1081); otherwise similar to *S. aucuparia*.

Spiraea albiflora — Japanese White Spirea

1082

Very handsome, low, rounded, dense, shrubby type (1082) with rich green summer foliage; large white flowers in June on new growth; of easy culture but not recommended for high-pH soils; nice mass, facer or grouping plant; prune in spring, since it flowers on new wood; 1½' high by 1½ to 2½' wide; Zone 4.

Spiraea bullata — Crispleaf Spirea

1083

Intriguing, low-mounded, ground cover shrub (1083); dark, almost blue-green summer foliage; deep rose-pink flowers in June; valuable dwarf shrub; 12 to 15'' high; Zone 4.

Spiraea x *bumalda* 'Anthony Waterer' — Anthony Waterer Bumald Spirea

1084

1085

1086

Mounded shrub (1084); new growth deep reddish purple, maturing to bluish green; flowers deep pink (1085) on new growth in June and throughout summer; widely used as a facer and for massing (1086), grouping; 2' by 3 to 4'; Zone 4.

Spiraea x *bumalda* 'Crispa'

1087

1088

Similar to 'Anthony Waterer', except leaves are twisted and serrations are deeply and finely cut (1087); probably not preferable to 'Anthony Waterer' but interesting because of textural difference; tends to be more open and floppy (1088); 2' by 3 to 4'; Zone 4.

Spiraea x *bumalda* 'Goldflame'

1089

Habit similar to 'Anthony Waterer'; new foliage mottled with red, copper and orange (1089), these colors repeated in the fall; pinkish flowers; 2½'; Zone 4.

Spiraea x bumalda 'Nyeswood'

1090

1091

1092

Very tight-knit, dense form with blue-green foliage; pink flowers in June; mounded shrub (1090) which lends itself to groupings (1091), low hedges (1092), massing; 15 to 18''; Zone 5.

Spiraea japonica — Japanese Spirea

1093

Bushy mounded grower (1093) with large, white, flat-topped flowers in June-July; at times somewhat untidy but a vigorous grower with rich green foliage and showy flowers; 3 to 5' by 4 to 6'; Zone 4.

Spiraea japonica 'Atrosanguinea' — Mikado Japanese Spirea

1094

Very handsome, upright-growing (1094) shrub with perhaps the deepest rose-red flowers of any spirea; 3 to 5' high; Zone 4.

Spiraea japonica var. *alpina* — Dwarf Alpine Spirea

1095

1096

1097

A very dainty, low-growing (1095) spirea; fine-textured, pink-flowered type; useful for facing (1096), massing (1097), ground cover; highly recommended; 12" high plant which spreads quite rapidly; Zone 4.

Spiraea nipponica 'Snowmound' — Snowmound Nippon Spirea

1098

1099

Rather stiff, upright, spreading shrub (1098); blue-green foliage; white flowers in May; uniform grower (1099); suitable for masses and hedges; preferable to *S.* x *vanhouttei*; 3 to 5' (7') high with a similar spread; Zone 4.

Spiraea prunifolia —Bridalwreath Spirea

1100

1101

1102

Upright, open, coarse, straggly shrub, often leggy (1100, 1101); foliage is lustrous dark green in summer, sometimes bronzed in fall; flowers are 1/3'' in diameter, double, white, mid to late April (1102); at one time a most popular plant, has lost favor and now belongs to the over-the-hill gang; 4 to 9' high by 6 to 8' wide; Zone 4.

Spiraea thunbergii — Thunberg Spirea

1103   1104

Bushy, slender-branched, tiny-leaved shrub, rather loosely spreading and arching, very twiggy (1103); foliage is yellowish green in summer, turning yellowish and tinged with orange and bronze in fall; small white flowers (1104) are borne on leafless stems in April; fine-textured plant, suitable for shrub border, valuable for early flowers; 3 to 5' by 3 to 5'; Zone 4.

Spiraea x *vanhouttei* — Vanhoutte Spirea

1105   1106

Extremely popular, old-fashioned shrub of fountain-like or vase-shaped outline; round-topped with branches recurving to ground, making a tall broad mound (1105); blue-green summer foliage; profuse white flowers (1106) in May; looks good in flower and foliage but rather gaunt and gaudy in winter; many better shrubs for modern landscapes; 8 to 10' by 10 to 12'; Zone 4.

Staphylea trifolia — American Bladdernut

1107

1108

1109

Weedy shrub, upright (1107), heavily branched; suckers and forms a solid aggregate of brush; sometimes wide-spreading; pale green summer foliage, dull yellow in fall; smooth striped bark; greenish white flowers (1108); interesting inflated seed capsule (1109); prefers shady, damp, moist areas; suitable for naturalizing; 10 to 15' with a similar or greater spread at maturity; Zone 3.

Stephanandra incisa — Cutleaf Stephanandra

1110

1111

1112

Graceful shrub with dense, fine-textured foliage and a distinct haystack (1110) to rounded outline; foliage is red-tinged when unfolding, later bright green, then red-purple to red-orange in fall; flowers are small, yellowish white; very adaptable plant with wide soil tolerance, however, often becomes chlorotic on high-pH soils; roots wherever stems touch moist soil; 'Crispa' (1111) is lower growing than species (1½ to 3'), otherwise similar; makes a good mass, curb cover (1112); tolerant of adverse conditions; functional durable plant; species grows 4 to 7' high with similar spread; Zone 4.

Stewartia pseudocamellia — Japanese Stewartia

1113

1114

1115

Large shrub (1113) or small tree (1114) with spreading branches and a bushy habit; foliage is a handsome dark green in summer, changing to beautiful orange and scarlet in fall; bark is singularly beautiful (1115), exfoliating to a sycamorish character but infinitely superior; white, 2 to 3" diameter flowers in July-August; requires moist acid soils, high in organic matter; superior specimen or shrub border plant; average landscape size would range from 20 to 35' in height; Zone 5.

Styrax japonicum — Japanese Snowbell

1116

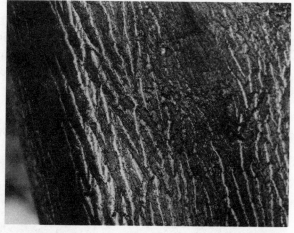

1119

1117

1120

1118

1121

Lovely, small, low-branched tree (1116) which develops a rounded to broad-rounded crown and a distinct horizontal appearance (1117); dark green summer foliage (1118), changing to yellow or reddish in fall but seldom good; handsome, gray-brown bark (1119) of smooth consistency but showing shallow interlacing fissures; beautiful, ¾'' diameter, bell-shaped flowers in June (1120); dry grayish drupes (1121) in August-September; requires acid, moist, well-drained soil and must be sited in a protected location in northern gardens; excellent patio tree, specimen, shrub border plant; one of the finest landscape trees; can grow 20 to 30' with a comparable spread; Zone 5, severely injured by −20 to −25°F during the winter of 1976-77.

Styrax obassium — Fragrant Snowbell

1122

1123

1124

Small tree (1122) or large shrub which develops dense ascending branches and forms an elliptical to weakly pyramidal outline; dark green summer foliage (1123); white fragrant flowers are borne in 4 to 8'' racemes (1124), June; not as effective as *S. japonicum* nor as hardy; 20 to 30'; Zone 6.

Symphoricarpos albus — Common Snowberry

1125

1126

1127

Bushy, irregular-growing shrub with numerous ascending shoots (1125); foliage is blue-green in summer and often develops a distinct lobed appearance (1126); flowers are pinkish, small, June; fruits are white, berry-like drupes (1127) which ripen sporadically from August through fall; adaptable plant, will grow on almost any soil, extremely shade-tolerant; 3 to 6' by 3 to 6'; Zone 3.

Symphoricarpos x *chenaultii* 'Hancock' — Hancock Chenault Coralberry

1128

1129

'Hancock' is a fine-textured, low-growing, ground cover shrub with bright green foliage; flowers are pinkish, fruits of pink-white color; makes a superlative wall cover (1128) or mass (1129); grows fast and fills in rapidly; good plant for difficult areas; 2' by 10 to 12'; Zone 4.

Symphoricarpos orbiculatus — Indian Currant Coralberry

1130

1131

Irregular, spreading, arching shrub, significantly suckering and developing large colonies (1130); blue-green summer foliage; yellowish white flowers, blushed rose; purplish red fruits cover the ends of the stems and persist into winter; grows anywhere and can become a noxious weed; extremely shade-tolerant; possibly used for naturalizing, otherwise limited use in modern landscapes; appears rather coarse in winter months (1131); 2 to 5' by 4 to 8'; Zone 2.

Syringa x *chinensis* — Chinese Lilac

1132

1133

A hybrid between *S. vulgaris* and *S. persica*; shrub is graceful, rounded to broad-spreading with arching branches (1132); more delicate in foliage and profuse in flower than *S. vulgaris*; flowers are lilac-purple, fragrant, mid-May, borne in 4 to 6" long panicles; can be extremely effective; will contract mildew; nice plant for screen (1133), shrub border, groupings, masses; 8 to 15'; Zone 4.

Syringa meyeri — Meyer Lilac
(also listed as *S. palibiniana* and *S. velutina*)

1134

Small, dense, neat, broad-mounded shrub (1134); dark green leaves with an orbicular shape and undulating margin; flowers are pinkish purple, fragrant, early to mid-May and may remain effective for 10 to 14 days; the entire shrub is literally masked by the flowers; makes a splendid shrub border plant, mass, grouping or informal hedge; buds emerge early and are often injured by late frosts; mildew free; 4 to 8' high, one and one-half times that in spread; Zone 4.

Syringa microphylla — Littleleaf Lilac

1135

1136

Very handsome, rounded to broad-spreading, densely branched shrub (1135); medium green summer foliage (1136); flowers are rosy lilac, fragrant, borne in small, 1½ to 2½'' long panicles in May through early June; may flower sporadically in summer and into fall; susceptible to mildew; worthwhile plant for border, groupings; 6 to 9' by 9 to 12'; Zone 4.

Syringa pekinensis — Pekin Lilac

1137

1138

1139

Similar in may respects to *S. reticulata* but smaller in size (15 to 20'), has a more informal, shrubby habit (1137) and finer textured leaves and stems; white flowers are borne in 3 to 6" wide panicles (1138) before those of *S. reticulata*; reddish brown bark (1139) separates into papery layers; excellent informal plant for the border; Zone 4.

Syringa persica — Persian Lilac

1140

1141

Graceful shrub of rounded outline (1140); foliage is a dark bluish green but often succumbs to mildew in the summer months; flowers are pale lilac, fragrant, mid-May, profusely borne; nice lilac for the shrub border (1141); 4 to 8' by 5 to 10'; Zone 5.

Syringa reticulata — Japanese Tree Lilac
(formerly *S. amurensis japonica*)

1142

1144

1143

Large shrub or small tree with stiff spreading branches, developing an oval to rounded crown (1142); dark green summer foliage; creamy white flowers are borne in 6 to 12″ long panicles (1143) in June; bark is a handsome reddish brown and resembles that of cherries; one of the easiest lilacs to culture; not as susceptible to insects and diseases as the common lilac; nice specimen plant for small landscapes (1144); 20 to 30′ by 15 to 25′; Zone 4.

Syringa villosa — Late or Summer Lilac

1145

Bushy shrub of dense habit with erect or ascending, stout, stiff branches (1145); medium green summer foliage; flowers vary from white to rosy lilac, late May into early June, with a privet-like odor; valuable lilac for extending the flowering season; the Preston hybrids are quite similar to *S. villosa* but offer a wider color range and larger flowers; species and hybrids are excellent border plants; 6 to 10' by 4 to 10'; Zone 2.

Syringa vulgaris — Common Lilac

1146

1147

1148

The granddaddy of lilacs; often over-planted in former years and has lost much favor in recent times because of large size and pest problems; upright leggy shrub of irregular outline, usually devoid of branches after a time and forming a cloud-like head (1146, 1147); blue-green summer foliage if not mildew-colored gray; lilac flowers of exceedingly fine scent in mid-May; quite susceptible to borers, scale, mildew; often overgrows the small property; can be used as an unpruned screen (1148) or shrub border plant; numerous cultivars, single or double flowered, ranging from white to amaranth-red in color; 8 to 15' (20') by 6 to 12' (15'); Zone 3.

Tamarix ramosissima — Five-stamen Tamarix (formerly *T. pentandra*)

1149

1150

1151

Usually a wild-growing, very loose, open shrub (1149); can be attractive with its fine-textured foliage (1150); light green, scale-like summer foliage creates a feathery appearance; rosy pink flowers (1151) are evident in July; very adaptable shrub for difficult sites, especially where salts present a problem; not recommended for the small residential landscape but perhaps good for highways and other difficult sites; 10 to 15' high, usually less in width; Zone 2.

Taxodium ascendens — Pondcypress

1156

1157

1158

Narrow-conical or columnar tree (1156) with spreading branches; a deciduous conifer; bright green, scale-like summer foliage (1157), changing to rich brown in autumn; very adaptable tree, withstanding wet and dry soils; very formal and stately (1158); must be properly used in the landscape; nice when used in groups near water; 70 to 80' by one-third that in spread; Zone 4.

Taxodium distichum — Common Baldcypress

1152

1155

1153

1154

A lofty deciduous conifer of slender pyramidal habit (1152, 1153), almost columnar in youth with a stout straight trunk buttressed at the base; short horizontal branches ascending at the ends, the lateral branches pendulous; bright, yellow-green foliage in spring, darkening in summer to a soft sage-green, becoming russet or soft brown in fall; bark (1154) is a reddish or orangish brown and develops a peeling characteristic; very adaptable to water (1155) and exists in swamps in its native haunts; will do well on drier soils but chlorosis can be a problem; worthwhile plant for low wet areas, along lakes and slow moving streams; 50 to 70' by 20 to 30'; Zone 4.

Taxus — Yew

1159

1160

The yews are a variable group of landscape plants (1159), differing principally in foliage colors (yellow to dark green) and habit (prostrate types to distinct columnar growers). The majority of the cultivars are derived from *T. cuspidata*, Japanese yew, and *T.* x *media*, Anglojap yew. Yews respond well to pruning and can be transformed into any shape. Plants such as those pictured (1160) are most effectively used in formal gardens.

Taxus baccata — English Yew

1161

1162

1163

The species is not effectively hardy in Zone 5, however, 'Repandens' (1161, 1162) is a hardy, dwarf, wide-spreading form with the tips of the branchlets pendulous, leaves flat and lustrous dark green above; 'Aurea' (1163) is a bushy compact form, branchlets yellow when young, leaves with yellow margins, changing to green during summer; like all *Taxus*, requires moist, well-drained soil for best growth; the species is a large tree or shrub; 36 to 60' high; Zone 6, except for 'Repandens'.

Taxus canadensis — Canadian or American Yew

1164

Often a prostrate, loose, straggling evergreen shrub when found in its native haunts, slightly more dense when open-grown (1164); not a choice landscape yew because the foliage assumes a reddish tint in winter; suitable as a ground cover but only for underplanting in cool shaded situations; 3 to 6' by 6 to 8', often rooting where the prostrate branches touch moist soil; Zone 2.

Taxus cuspidata — Japanese Yew

1165

1166

1167

1169

1168

Crown erect or flattened, broad or narrow, of irregular habit with spreading or upright-spreading branches (1165); dark green, evergreen foliage; on female plants the fleshy, red-coated seeds (1166) are ornamental; variety *capitata* (1167, 1168) is a pyramidal form which assumes tree-like proportions; yews are often thought of as small, diminutive foundation plants, but with time they can effectively overgrow a house (1169) unless properly pruned; there are many cultivars of *T. cuspidata* and it is prudent to check with the local nurseryman for the best types for your area; 10 to 40' with an equal or greater spread; Zone 4.

Taxus x *media* — Anglojap Yew

1170

1171

1172

1173

1174

1175

1176
1177

The species is a misnomer since various plants were selected from crosses between *T. baccata* and *T. cuspidata* and given cultivar names. The following are limitedly representative of the cultivars at one's landscape disposal: 'Brownii' (1170), a male clone with a densely rounded habit, foliage dark green, 9' high by 12' wide after 15 years; 'Chadwickii' (1171), valuable, low-growing, broad-spreading clone with excellent dark green foliage; 'Hatfieldii' (1172), a male clone, dense, broad-pyramidal, leaves dark green, 12' high by 10' wide after 20 years, excellent for screens and hedging (1173); 'Hicksii' (1174), male and female clones, distinctly columnar in form, widely used as a hedge (1175), screen and foundation plant, 20' high after 15 to 20 years; 'Wardii' (1176), wide-spreading, dense form with extremely dark green foliage, 6' high by 19' wide after 20 years; to emphasize the inherent problems with yew identification, I have included this photograph (1177) of *eight* different upright clones of *T.* x *media*—there is not an iota's difference among them; Zone 4.

Thuja occidentalis — American Arborvitae

1179

1178

1180   1181

A dense, narrow to broad-pyramidal (1178) evergreen with short ascending branches to the ground which end in flat, spreading, horizontal sprays; flat green in summer, changing to yellow-brown-green in winter; adaptable evergreen, very tolerant of moist and dry soils, including those of limestone origin; makes a good specimen plant, grouping (1179), hedge (1180); often over-used in the landscape because of ease of culture; 'Techny' and 'Nigra' maintain good, dark green foliage all winter; 'Woodwardii' (1181) is a globose form, wider than high, foliage dark green in summer, often browning slightly in winter; 40 to 60' high by 10 to 15' (20') wide; Zone 2.

Thuja orientalis — Oriental Arborvitae
(*Platycladus orientalis* according to *Hortus III*)

1182

A large shrub or small tree of dense, compact, conical or oval habit (1182); branches held vertically when young; becoming in age loose and open and not so markedly vertical; composed of many slender branches which tend to bend and break in snow; bright yellow-green to grass-green foliage in youth, changing to a lustrous darker green at maturity; not a good plant for the midwest or east but often used in southwest; appears exceedingly tolerant of hot dry climates and alkaline soils; 18 to 25' high by 10 to 12' wide; best in Zone 6, however, often planted in Zone 5.

Thuja plicata — Giant or Western Arborvitae

1183

Similar to *T. occidentalis* in most respects (1183); supposedly maintains good, dark green foliage throughout the season; valuable landscape tree; 50 to 75' by 15 to 25'; can grow 180 to 200' in northwestern United States where it is native; Zone 5.

Thymus serphyllum — Mother-of-Thyme

1184

1185

Prostrate weak shrub or nearly herbaceous perennial; spreading, trailing, with rooting stems (1184); medium green summer foliage, although the numerous cultivars, as well as other species, offer grayish, bluish, yellowish green, whitish-margined and yellowish-colored foliage; flowers are rose-purple, June through September; makes a beautiful, carpet-like effect when in flower; nice plant for edging (1185), rock walls and dry places; seems to perform better under poor dry soil conditons; high fertility results in rampant unregulated growth; 1 to 3" high, spreading indefinitely; Zone 4.

Tilia americana — American Linden

1186

1187

1188

Tall stately tree (1186) with numerous, slender, low-hung, spreading branches; pyramidal in youth; at maturity the lower branches droop down, (1187) then curve up, forming a deep, ovate, oblong crown; dark green summer foliage, leaves often develop a brownish cast in late August or September and actually become unsightly; pale yellow, fragrant flowers in mid to late June; in general not a tree for the residential landscape, though interesting in a native situation; 'Fastigiata' (1188) is a distinct pyramidal form for restricted growing areas; 60 to 80' in height with a spread of one-half to two-thirds the height; Zone 2.

Tilia cordata — Littleleaf Linden

1189

1190

1191

Pyramidal in youth (1189); upright-oval (1190) to broad-pyramidal (1191) at maturity; dark green summer foliage, seldom any trace of yellow in fall; fragrant yellowish flowers in late June or July; the most popular linden in modern landscaping because of transplanting ease, pollution tolerance and adaptability to restricted growing areas, including city streets and planters; many excellent cultivars ('Chancellor', 'Greensprire', 'June Bride') are available; makes a fine lawn or specimen tree; 60 to 70' high with a spread of one-half to two-thirds that; Zone 3.

Tilia x *euchlora* — Crimean Linden

1192

1194

1193

Similar to *T. cordata* in habit (1192); differs by virture of the lustrous dark green leaves, which show distinct mucronate teeth on their margins (1193), and offers perhaps the best foliage of any linden; often suckers profusely from the base (due to grafting), creating a maintenance problem; 'Redmond' (1194) is a supposed hybrid between *T.* x *euchlora* and *T. americana* with larger, less glossy leaves than *T.* x *euchora*: very vigorous tree, finding much favor in the midwest; 40 to 60' high and one-half that in width; Zone 4.

Tilia heterophylla — Beetree or White Linden

1195

Similar to *T. americana* in many features; perhaps a better landscape tree (1195); undersides of the leaves are whitish or sometimes brownish tomentose; 60 to 80' high; Zone 5.

Tilia petiolaris — Pendent Silver Linden

1196

1197

Closely allied to *T. tomentosa* but differing in the pedulous branching habit (1196, 1197); bees supposedly find the flowers narcotic or poisonous, but I have not observed this on the campus tree; lovely specimen; 60' by about half that in spread; Zone 5.

Tilia tomentosa — Silver Linden

1198

1199

Pyramidal when young (1198), upright-oval to rounded in old age (1199); foliage is a lustrous dark green above and a silvery white beneath; quite effective when buffeted about by the wind; fragrant yellowish flowers are effective in late June through early July; this and *T. petiolaris* are the last species to flower in central Illinois; makes a superb specimen tree; 50 to 70' by one-half to two-thirds that in width; Zone 4.

Tsuga canadensis — Canadian Hemlock

1200

1201

1202

1203

1204

Softly and gracefully pyramidal in youth with tapering trunk, becoming pendulously pyramidal with age (1200); dark, glossy green needles, lower sides having two glaucous bands; bark is a handsome brown; prefers moist, sandy or rocky, well-drained soils and should be protected from winter sun and desiccating winds; hemlock forests (1201) cast such dense shade that other plants are unable to compete; one of the premier evergreens for landscape use in the northeastern states; makes an excellent specimen, grouping, informal screen or hedge (1202); responds to pruning as well as any conifer; 'Pendula' ('Sargentii') is the most popular cultivar and forms a broad weeping mound of cascading branches (1203, 1204); 40 to 70' by 25 to 35'; Zone 3.

Tsuga caroliniana — Carolina Hemlock

1205

Airy, spire-topped tree with a tapering trunk and short, stout, often pendulous branches forming a handsome, evenly pyramidal head (1205); glossy, dark green needles; supposedly performs better than *T. canadensis* under city conditions but will never supersede it in popularity; 45 to 60' by 20 to 25'; Zone 4.

Ulmus americana — American Elm

1206

1207

1208

1209

1210

Perhaps the most famous of native North American trees; once widely planted in cities throughout its native range, it has suffered the ravages of Dutch elm disease and phloem necrosis and can no longer be safely recommended; most common form is that of vase-shaped outline (1206), trunk divided into several erect limbs which are strongly arched above and terminate in numerous, slender, often pendulous branchlets; the whole tree a picture of great beauty and symmetry (1207, 1208); foliage is a lustrous, dark green in summer, often changing to good yellow in fall; American Elm was often planted on either side of walks or streets to create a "cathedral ceiling" effect (1209); a fine specimen tree but an unfortunate illustration of the fact that extensive use of one tree often results in disasterous effects when a specific pathogen or insect becomes serious; 'Ascendens' (1210) is an upright-oval clone useful for screening but is susceptible to Dutch elm disease; 60 to 80' with a spread of one-half to two-thirds the height; Zone 2.

Ulmus carpinifolia — Smoothleaf Elm

1211

1212

Weakly pyramidal tree (1211), usually developing a straight trunk and slender ascending branches; glossy, dark green, summer foliage; no real value in North American landscapes because there are so many superior trees; some of the new Dutch elm disease-resistant clones have come from hybridization with *U. carpinifolia* but are scarcely worth considering; 'Umbraculifera' (1212) is a vase or globe-shaped tree of limited worth; 70 to 90' by 35 to 45'; Zone 4.

Ulmus glabra — Scotch Elm

1213

1214

1215

The species is seldom seen in cultivation but is represented by the cultivars 'Camperdownii' (1213) and 'Pendula' (1214) (now listed as 'Horizontalis'); 'Camperdownii' is gracefully drooping, forming a globose head and is usually top-worked on erect elm stock; 'Pendula' has stiffly drooping branches, more or less elbowed, making a horizontal spreading crown; the intricate branchwork makes an ideal snow collector (1215); both cultivars are worthy of consideration, though susceptible to numerous insects and diseases; the foliage is a rough, flat, dark, bluish green on both; Zone 4.

Ulmus parvifolia — Chinese Elm

1216

1217

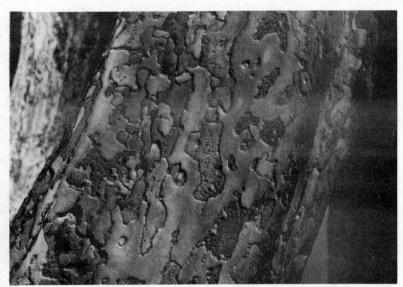

1219

1218

Usually a broad, round-topped tree with fine branches and small leaves (1216, 1217); dark green summer foliage which may turn yellow or reddish in fall (seldom does); flowers in the fall while most elms flower in spring; most outstanding attribute is the bark, which on older trunks (1218, 1219) develops a beautiful mottled combination of green, gray, orange and brown areas; this species should not be confused with *U. pumila* (Siberian Elm), which is a much inferior tree; makes a nice small specimen tree; 40 to 50' by 40 to 50'; Zone 5.

Ulmus pumila — Siberian Elm

1220

1221

Perhaps the worst tree on the green earth; the habit is rather open, usually with several large ascending branches with flexible, pendulous, breakable branchlets (1220, 1221); summer foliage is dark green and cherished by foliar-feeding insects; this tree does not deserve to be planted anywhere; messy, extremely weak-wooded, absolutely no redeeming ornamental characteristics other than *fast* growth; 50 to 70' high, three-fourth's that in spread; Zone 4.

Vaccinium corymbosum — Highbush Blueberry

1222

1223

1224

1225

Upright multistemmed shrub with spreading branches, forming a rounded, dense, compact outline (1222), especially under cultivation; lustrous, dark green to bluish green summer foliage (1223), changing to yellow, bronze, orange, red and purple in the fall; white, often tinged pink, urn-shaped flowers (1224) are borne in May; the blue-black, juicy berries (1225) mature in July-August; requires an acid moist soil; makes an excellent shrub border plant, providing a good crop of fruits as well as having outstanding ornamental characteristics; determine the cultivars best suited for your area; 6 to 12' by 8 to 12'; Zone 3.

Viburnum acerifolium — Mapleleaf Viburnum

1226

1227

A low-growing, sparsely branched shrub, often of a straggly nature (1226); bright to dark green summer foliage, changing to an interesting pinkish red or reddish purple in fall; white flowers (1227), black fruit, both limitedly ornamental; excellent plant for shady moist areas; effective in naturalizing; 4 to 6' by 3 to 4'; Zone 3.

Viburnum x *burkwoodii* — Burkwood Viburnum

1228

1229

Upright, multistemmed, often tangled mass of stems (1228), yielding an irregular oval to haystack outline; leaves are lustrous, dark green above, gray-brown tomentose beneath in summer and may turn wine-red in fall (usually do not); flowers are pink in bud, white when open, sensuously fragrant, 2 to 3'' across, April; fruits are red, changing to black and sparsely produced; like most viburnums, enjoys a moist, well-drained, slightly acid soil; handsome plant for early spring flower and fragrance; works well in groups (1229), shrub borders, even foundations if properly pruned; 8 to 10' high and about two-thirds that in width; Zone 5.

Viburnum carlesii — Koreanspice Viburnum

1230

1231

1232

Rounded dense shrub with stiff, upright, spreading branches (1230, 1231); dull, dark green summer foliage, reddish to wine-red in fall but not consistent; flowers are pink to red in bud, opening white, exceedingly fragrant, borne in a 2 to 3″ diameter hemispherical cyme, late April to early May; very popular landscape plant because of spicy aromatic flowers; fruit is seldom effective; use as foundation plant, in groupings, masses; 'Compactum' (1232) grows about one-half the size of the species, nice plant for the small landscape; 4 to 8′ by 4 to 8′; Zone 4.

Viburnum cassinoides — Witherod Viburnum

1233

1234

A handsome dense shrub, compact and rounded with spreading, finally slightly arching branches (1233); lustrous green summer foliage, changing to orange-red, dull crimson and purple in fall; large, 5'' diameter white flowers in June, followed by fruits which change from pink to red to blue, before becoming black in September (1234); a very lovely but little-used shrub which has a place in natural-izing, massing and the shrub border; 5 to 6' (10') with a similar spread; Zone 2.

Viburnum dentatum — Arrowwood Viburnum

1235

1236

1237

One of the most dependable viburnums; multistemmed, dense, rounded shrub (1235), often with spreading, finally arching branches; lustrous green in summer foliage, ranging from yellow through glossy red to reddish purple in fall; white flowers in late May to early June; bluish black fruits (1236) in September which are relished by the birds; valued for durability and utility; effective in hedges, screens (1237), groupings, masses and as a filler in the shrub border; 6 or 8 to 15' by 6 to 15'; Zone 2.

Viburnum dilatatum — Linden Viburnum

1238

1239

1240

In best form, a dense rounded shrub (1238, 1239) of rather neat proportions; foliage is lustrous, dark green in summer, changing to inconsistent orangish brown or russet-red in fall; white flowers in late May to early June; superior, cherry-red fruit (1240), maturing in September-October and often persisting into December; fruit is by far the most spectacular characteristic; same uses as *V. dentatum*; 8 to 10' high, two-thirds to equal that in width; Zone 4.

Viburnum farreri — Fragrant Viburnum

1241

1243

1242

Variable shrub (1241), usually with some horizontal branch development, however, may tend towards a rounded outline; dark green summer foliage, changing to reddish purple in fall; flowers are pinkish, lusciously fragrant, borne on leafless stems in early April (1242); often flowers in the fall; fruit colors red, finally black; worthwhile plant for early fragrance; 'Nanum' (1243) is a dwarf form, growing 2 to 3' by 4 to 6'; species grows 8 to 12' high with an irregular spread; Zone 5.

Viburnum lantana — Wayfaringtree Viburnum

1244

1245

Multistemmed shrub with stout spreading branches, oval to rounded in outline (1244); dark green summer foliage; white flowers in early to mid-May; yellow to red to black fruit (1245), often all colors present in the same infructescence (cluster), August to September; very tolerant of calcareous soils; used for hedges, screens, massing, shrub border; one of the coarsest viburnums; 10 to 15' by 10 to 15'; Zone 3.

Viburnum lentago — Nannyberry Viburnum, Sheepberry

1246

1247

Large shrub or small tree with slender, finally arching branches (1246), somewhat open at maturity, often suckering; foliage soft yellow green when unfolding, changing to glossy green and easily separated from *V. prunifolium* by winged petiole (1247); fall color is purplish red but inconsistent; flowers are white in mid-May, followed by blue-black fruits in September-October; ideal shrub for naturalizing, as a background; tends to sucker and requires considerable room; may contract mildew which detracts from appearance; 15 to 18' (possibly 30') high, spread variable; Zone 2.

Viburnum opulus — European Cranberrybush Viburnum

1248

1249

1250

1251

1252

1253

Upright-spreading shrub of oval to rounded outline (1248); glossy, dark green summer foliage, changing to yellow-red and reddish purple in autumn; flowers are borne in flat-topped cymes (1249), the outer white flowers sterile and showy, the inner fertile; fruit is bright red (1250), undergoes several color transformations from yellow to red and is often persistent through winter; very easily cultured shrub and widely offered by nurserymen; too large for the small landscape but ideal for large shrub borders, screens, groupings; 'Compactum' (1251) is an excellent plant where space is limited, one-half the size of the species and extremely dense, flowering and fruiting abundantly; 'Nanum' (1252) is a dwarf form, much branched, 18 to 24" high; 'Roseum' (1253) is an old-fashioned form with snowball-like flowers, handsome in flower but very susceptible to aphids and flowers are sterile, hence, no fruit; species 8 to 12' (15') by 10 to 15'; Zone 3.

Viburnum plicatum — Japanese Snowball Viburnum

1254

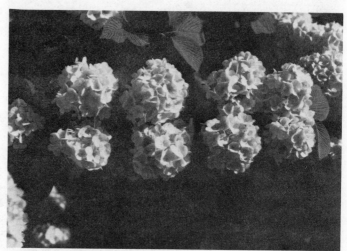

1255

1256

More upright than variety *tomentosum* but still displaying a slight horizontal branching habit (1254); dark green summer foliage, reddish purple fall coloration; white, sterile, 2 to 3" diameter, snowball-shaped flowers in May (1255); worthwhile plant for the flower effect; is not as significantly susceptible to aphids as *V. o.* 'Roseum' and for that reason is preferred; good plant for shrub border; 'Grandiflorum' (1256) is a profusely flowered form; 8 to 12' high; Zone 4.

Viburnum plicatum var. *tomentosum* — Doublefile Viburnum

Perhaps the loveliest of the viburnums when properly grown; distinct, horizontal, tiered branches (1257, 1258) create a stratified effect, the whole shrub appearing rounded to broad-rounded at maturity; foliage color similar to that of the species; excellent flowers, similar to *V. opulus* (1259) but raised above the foliage (1260) and two-ranked along the stem (hence the name, "Doublefile"); fruit (1261) is an excellent cherry-red and changes to black at maturity, though birds usually strip the plant before it ripens completely; choice specimen plant for foundations, borders, screens, massing; 8 to 10′ by 9 to 12′; Zone 4.

Viburnum prunifolium — Blackhaw Viburnum

1262

1264

1263

Round-headed tree (1262) or multistemmed shrub, stiffly branched, similar to *Crataegus* in growth habit; dark green summer foliage (1263); fall color varies from purple to red; profuse white flowers in May (1264); bluish black, sweetish fruits in September which may be eaten raw or made into preserves; very adaptable plant, withstands extremes of soil, sun or shade; nice small specimen tree, shrub border plant; 12 to 15' by 8 to 12'; Zone 3.

Viburnum rhytidophylloides — Lantanaphyllum Viburnum

1265

1266

Upright-spreading shrub with slightly arching branches, forming a haystack to rounded outline (1265, 1266); leathery, dark green foliage in summer; whitish flowers in May, followed by red to black fruits in August-September; easily grown, much hardier than *V. rhytidophyllum*; good screen, shrub border plant; 8 to 10′ (and larger) with a similar spread; Zone 4.

Viburnum rhytidophyllum — Leatherleaf Viburnum

1268

1267

1269

Upright, strongly multistemmed shrub, often somewhat open with age, usually upright-oval to rounded in outline (1267, 1268); dark green, lustrous, leathery summer foliage; creamy flowers in May, buds of which are formed the year prior to flowering (1269); fruit may be a good red going to black; this species and the previous one are apparently self-sterile—I have seen plants with no fruit and others abundantly endowed; good plant for foliage but may winter-kill in −15°F weather; 10 to 15′ with a similar spread; Zone 6.

Viburnum sargentii — Sargent Viburnum

1270

1271

Multistemmed, upright-rounded to rounded shrub of relatively coarse texture (1270), somewhat similar to *V. opulus* and *V. trilobum* but not as handsome; flowers and fruits are similar to *V. opulus* (1271); 12 to 15′ by 12 to 15′; Zone 4.

Viburnum setigerum — Tea Viburnum

1273

1272

Has perhaps the worst growth habit of the viburnums but certainly worth considering for fruit; upright, multistemmed, often leggy at the base (1272); flat, soft, blue-green summer foliage (1273); small, flat-topped, cymose, white flowers in May; red fruit (1/3″ long) which persists into fall; probably should be used only in the shrub border; 8 to 12′ high, two-thirds that in width; Zone 5 (4).

Viburnum sieboldii — Siebold Viburnum

1274

1275

1276

Large shrub or small tree of open habit with stout, stiff, rigid branches (1274); often quite picturesque when limbed-up and allowed to spread; handsome, glossy, bright green foliage; creamy white
flowers (1275) in late May which yield rose-red (1276), finally black fruits in September; the inflo-
rescences are a handsome rose-red and remain effective after the fruit is eaten by the birds; one of
the finest large viburnums; use as a specimen, against large buildings, in groupings, border; must be
seen throughout the seasons to be fully appreciated; 15 to 20' (30') by 10 to 15'; Zone 4.

Viburnum trilobum — American Cranberrybush Viburnum

1278

1277

1279

Similar to *V. opulus* in most respects except petiole morphology; could be considered the American counterpart of *V. opulus* (1277, 1278); 'Compactum' (1279) is an especially handsome, oval-rounded form with good flowering and fruiting qualities, about one-half the size of the species; 8 to 12' by 8 to 12'; Zone 2.

Vinca minor — Common Periwinkle

1280   1281

Low-growing, prostrate, mat-forming, evergreen ground cover (1280); lustrous green foliage throughout the seasons if properly sited; lilac-blue, 1" diameter flowers (1281) in March-April; prefers moist, loose, well-drained soil and a shady location; siting in full sun in the midwest results in foliage discoloration; one of the superb evergreen ground covers for shady areas; 3 to 6" high, rooting where the stems touch moist soil and spreading indefinitely; Zone 4.

Vitex negundo var. *heterophylla* — Cutleaf Chastetree

1282   1283

Develops a loosely branched, airy, open outline (1282) but is so often frozen to the ground in northern states that it reacts like an herbaceous perennial (1283); grayish green summer foliage; lilac or lavender flowers in August; prefers well-drained, loose, open, sunny areas; best used in the shrub border; 3 to 5' in a single season when injured the previous winter, may reach 15' in height; Zone 6.

Weigela florida — Old-fashioned Weigela

1285

1284

1286

Spreading, dense, rounded shrub (1284) with coarse branches which eventually arch to the ground; medium green summer foliage; rosy pink, tubular flowers (1285) in late May to early June and sporadically on current season's growth thereafter; readily adaptable but requires well-drained soil and full sun; shrub border plant only, since it possesses only a single period of interest; 'Variegata' (1286) has leaves edged with yellow, makes a rather nauseous sight in the garden; 6 to 9' by 9 to 12'; Zone 5.

Wisteria floribunda — Japanese Wisteria

1287

1288

1289

1290

Perhaps the most beautiful of all flowering vines; stout vine, climbing by twining stems (1287), developing twisted woody trunks (1288); often requires considerable support which should not be of wood origin; dark green summer foliage; violet or violet-blue flowers are borne in slender, 8 to 20″ racemes in May; exceedingly beautiful in flower (1289); requires considerable cultural care; valuable vine for trellises (1290), walls and anywhere there is ample support; 30′ or more; Zone 4. *Wisteria sinensis* is similar but has fewer leaflets (usually 11) and the flowers open simultaneously.

Xanthorhiza simplicissima — Yellowroot

1292

1291

Flat-topped ground cover with erect stems and celery-like leaves, filling the ground as a mat (1291); lustrous green foliage in summer, changing to golden yellow and orange in fall; brownish purple flowers (1292) are borne on leafless stems in April; prefers moist, organic, well-drained soils and partial shade; excellent ground cover for moist shady areas; 1 to 2′ high, spreading indefinitely; Zone 4.

Zelkova serrata — Japanese Zelkova

1293

1294

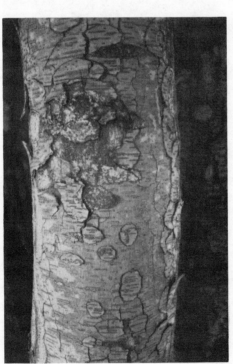

1295

In youth a low-branched, vase-shaped tree (1293); in old age maintaining a similar form (1294) with many ascending branches; dark green summer foliage, changing to yellow-orange-brown in fall (possibly wine-red); bark is reddish brown and cherry-like in youth, often becoming mottled (1295) like *Ulmus parvifolia* in old age; of easy culture compared to the elms and for this reason recommended; handsome tree for shade, street, park or golf course; 50 to 80' high with an equal spread; Zone 5.

SCIENTIFIC NAME INDEX